Artificial Stone

Artificial Stone

A successful substitute for natural stone?

Simon Scott MA

This work is dedicated to the memory of
my dear Mother
who encouraged me to embark on my studies
yet did not live to see their conclusion.

By the same author:
Formula One Drivers' Profiles, 1982
The Follies of Boughton Park, 1995

First published in 2009 by:

HADDONSTONE LTD
The Forge House, East Haddon
Northampton NN6 8DB England

Telephone: 01604 770711
Fax: 01604 770027
publishing@haddonstone.co.uk
www.haddonstone.com

ISBN 978-0-9563891-0-7

Cover: Haddonstone's Jubilee urn, adapted from a Blashfield original

Contents

Acknowledgements .... Page 4

Introduction .... Page 6

Chapter I: Clay or Cement? .... Page 12

Chapter II: Coade's Pre-eminence. .... Page 25

Chapter III: The Nineteenth-century Followers. .... Page 41

Chapter IV: Manufacturers since World War II .... Page 57

Chapter V: Perceptions Through Three Centuries .... Page 81

Conclusion .... Page 99

Endnotes .... Page 104

Bibliography .... Page 111

Acknowledgements

A work such of this could not have happened without the help of others. Firstly, I offer my sincere thanks to my fellow directors at Haddonstone, in particular David Barrow and Adrian Coles, who were most supportive during my studies. And to Miranda Eldridge, my PA, whose invaluable assistance has helped to transform my words into the volume you see today.

This work is based on my dissertation submitted for an MA course at the University of Leicester entitled: 'The Country House: Art History and Literature' for which I was awarded a pass with distinction. I would like to thank those at the University who were particularly helpful and encouraging during my studies including Professor Phillip Lindley, Dr Sophie Oosterwijk, Professor Rosemary Sweet, Dr Susan Gordon and Carol Charles. Also, to Dr Simon Richards, my Dissertation Supervisor, who made numerous helpful comments when this work was at its draft stage.

The greatest debt of gratitude goes to those who foolishly volunteered to proof read my dissertation before submission: Michael Cousins and James Hasler. Michael is a wonderful font of information on all manner of landscape history matters whom I first came to know through The Folly Fellowship when I campaigned to save Boughton Park from a bypass and a quarry. James is my former English master at Wellingborough School whose knowledge of English usage is, in my opinion, second to none. Any errors, however, remain the sole responsibility of the author.

The principal archives consulted during research for the dissertation were those of the British Library, National Archives, National Art Library at the Victoria & Albert Museum, Royal Horticultural Society Lindley Library, Royal Institute of British Architects, Stamford Museum Archives, and Haddonstone Archives. The latter presented a rich vein of material that has not previously been studied or chronicled.

As a Director of Haddonstone Ltd, I have been allowed unrestricted access to the company's archives that contain much commercially sensitive information. For that reason this invaluable resource would not normally be available for study. The company also has an extensive library with volumes dating to the early-eighteenth century. My position at Haddonstone - where I have been responsible for the company's marketing, library and archives since 1989 - undoubtedly served to foster my genuine passion for the subject matter of my dissertation.

Foremost among the secondary reference sources was undoubtedly *Antique Garden Ornament* by John Davis, who kindly allowed me full access to his comprehensive archives and even read through a draft of my dissertation. Even Davis acknowledges that 'Relatively little research has been done on artificial stone'. Indeed, the only significant volume on any of the manufacturers in the field of artificial stone is Alison Kelly's seminal work, *Mrs Coade's Stone*. For amusement, nothing can surpass Richard Holt's *A Short Treatise of Artificial Stone* dating from 1730. It is a wonderful volume which allowed me to read, at first hand, the impassioned words of the first known exponent of artificial stone in modern times – being at times passionate, erudite, naïve, even ridiculous. Whilst there are many general works on the subject of garden ornamentation, few are of truly academic value. Everything else has proved to be a fascinating jigsaw of contemporary and secondary material.

Thanks are due to many others who have provided information and advice including: Eric Lennox, Alison Lowe and Neil Sparrow at Haddonstone; Gaynor Gilbert of Chilstone; Christopher Gallagher and Julian Gibbs at the National Trust; John Stewart and Jenifer White at English Heritage; Duncan Ellison for his ceramics advice; Richard Funnell for permission to quote from his thesis; Annabel Downs and Kate Lander at the Landscape Institute; Philip Norman at the Museum of Garden History; Stephen Astley at Sir John Soane's Museum; and, Christopher Marsden at the Victoria and Albert Museum Archives. I also gratefully acknowledge the individuals and organisations who have kindly allowed me to reproduce their images which add so much to this work.

Simon Scott, September 2009

Introduction

Artificial stone, or cast stone as it is most commonly called today, has a long and illustrious history that intertwines with the great boom in classically inspired country house building from the eighteenth century onwards. There have been more imitations of stone than of any other natural building material. This persistent emulation has most consistently been for reasons of economy, availability and fashion – particularly in applications where quarried stone is difficult, time-consuming and forbiddingly expensive to employ. In the eighteenth century, designs created by leading manufacturers were used at prestigious country house locations such as Belton, Burghley, Croome, Ickworth, Kedleston and Stowe whilst artificial stone today is still being used to enhance country houses across the nation, from Mount Edgcumbe in Cornwall to Aske Hall in Northumberland.

Reproduced by kind permission of Haddonstone Archives

Artificial-stone balustrading at the Grade I listed Aske Hall

One of the key attributes of artificial stone is that it takes on the appearance of natural stone, making it very difficult to distinguish from its quarried equivalent. This may be the reason why very few studies have specifically examined artificial stone. Certainly, no studies have been made which specifically look at the perceptions of artificial stone across the last three centuries and none have looked at the key manufacturers of the late-twentieth century. This work aims to correct such significant oversights.

Artificial stone is, confusingly, referred to by many different names, including: art stone, simulated stone, substitute stone, faux stone, manufactured stone, reconstructed stone, reconstituted stone, composite stone, fabricated stone, patent stone, composition stone, cement fondue, cast stone, even terracotta and concrete. Some commentators try to distinguish between twentieth-century composite or cast stone and products of earlier times, which are more frequently referred to as artificial stone. For simplicity and to avoid unnecessary confusion, for the purposes of this work, the term 'artificial stone' is used throughout, unless another term is used in a quotation.

This volume aims to provide a history of the most important manufacturers of artificial stone from the eighteenth century to the present day, mainly from the perspective of garden or landscape ornamentation: Coade, Blashfield, Austin & Seeley, Doulton, Pulham, Chilstone and Haddonstone. This work is not intended to be an all-embracing account of every artificial stone producer. Chapter I identifies clay and cement-based manufacturing as the two principal methods for the creation of artificial stone, including contemporary accounts of these two widely used alternatives to natural stone. Chapter II reviews the principal artificial stone manufacturers from the early-eighteenth century to the mid-nineteenth century, a period dominated by the Coade company. Chapter III examines the manufacturers who succeeded Coade from the mid nineteenth through to the early-twentieth century, focussing on Blashfield, Austin & Seeley, Doulton and Pulham. Chapter IV looks at the revival in artificial stone manufacturing from the Second World War to the present, principally through the works of Chilstone and Haddonstone. Having reviewed the alternative manufacturing processes for artificial stone as well as the development of the manufacturers themselves, Chapter V explores both historical and contemporary perceptions of artificial stone over the last three hundred years, thereby identifying both changes and similarities in opinion relating to this sometimes controversial material. This chapter is key to the work as it chronicles the debate that has run from the eighteenth century to the present as to the acceptability of artificial stone.

Advocates of artificial stone have constantly had to rebuff a series of attacks and assertions which are normally unsubstantiated – the material being derogatorily referred to by some as dishonest, makeshift, mean and a dismal sham. At the end of the twentieth century a leading architect, Terry Farrell, gave a flavour for the dichotomy of views, which this work will attempt to uncover:

> *I have used reconstructed stone on many buildings […] It is a useful material, but the very name raises an important issue in modern architecture. There is a very distinct difference in how some architects perceive reconstructed stone; one group is looking for an imitation of natural stone to use contextually; another group – one might call them the die-hard modernists – would not contemplate any imitation of stone, though they might happily accept a material known as pre-cast which is coloured and has a surface texture. Of course, the two materials are one and the same […] As a practice we are interested in reconstructed stone because it extends the possibilities of architectural expression to include an industrial heavyweight material […] And if you are searching for a completely modern material, precision-made, which has weight, 'gravitas' and permanence, you will find these qualities in reconstructed stone.[2]*

This work attempts to engage with this fascinating debate by quoting and commenting on a wide variety of published and unpublished contemporary sources.

* * * * * *

Before looking in detail at the history and perceptions of artificial stone, it would be helpful to provide the reader with a brief overview of the key movements and individuals in the history of garden ornamentation and landscape design. These impact directly on the demand for artificial stone through the centuries. Such an overview also provides useful historical context for this under-researched area of study.

As early as the mid-sixteenth century, gardens in England were increasingly influenced by the Renaissance styles from the Continent, with terraces being decorated with balustrading and statuary, although England never fully accepted the grand formality of the French. By the mid-seventeenth century, the fashion for garden sculpture had spread northwards across Europe from Italy, along with Italian designers and craftsmen. As a consequence, elaborate formal gardens soon appeared across France, Germany and the Netherlands, richly adorned with figures of gods and goddesses, shepherds and shepherdesses, nymphs and satyrs. In England, many of the early ornaments were specially commissioned sculptures featuring heraldic animals. Examples can be found at the royal palaces of the Tudors. Not all of these early garden ornaments were purely decorative. For example, sundials, wellheads and cisterns had both decorative and practical functions.

The materials used for garden ornaments reflected the fashion of the time and the climate of the country. Marble, for example, although widely used in Italy, will not survive unprotected through harsh English winters. For this reason, local stone such as Portland stone became prized for its suitability to the English climate. Initially, the cheapest of all materials was lead, which was often painted to resemble stone. The Industrial Revolution brought new methods of mass production, including cast iron designs by the likes of Coalbrookdale and Britannia Ironworks from the nineteenth century onwards. Parallel with this was the development of artificial stone. Mass-produced from moulds, garden ornaments spread to a much wider market during the nineteenth and twentieth centuries, as the desire to own a small piece of our classical heritage spread from grand landscapes to much more modest gardens.

In 1728, Batty Langley declared that 'nothing adds so much to the Beauty and Grandeur of Gardens, as fine Statues'.[3] Consequently, ornaments became a well-established part of the designed English landscape through the seventeenth, eighteenth and nineteenth centuries owing to the influence of the Grand Tour, amongst other factors. The urn became an object of universal admiration in eighteenth century England, as the shape satisfied the Palladian ideal for proportion, thereby recalling the classical perfection of the ancients. Urns at this time were never planted; planting of them was a Victorian introduction. With so many landowners and, in some instances, their landscape designers travelling to France and Italy in particular, the desire to embellish one's country seat with statuary and ornament in the classical style proved vital to the ultimate development of the artificial stone industry. The illustrious designers of these times – such as Kent, Vanbrugh, Brown and Repton – all acknowledged the importance of ornaments to embellish their designs, whether formal garden or sweeping landscape. By the second half of the eighteenth century, most landowners were sweeping away the great formal layouts that existed around their houses. The vogue for statuary and urns returned in the nineteenth century with the designs of Sir Charles Barry, Sir Joseph Paxton and William Nesfield. Equally, with an expanding middle class, the desire for garden ornamentation increased and artificial stone manufacturers thrived. In effect, classical, Renaissance and French Baroque styles could all be produced in almost limitless quantities and thus most garden ornaments were no longer the exclusive privilege of the rich.

Grand Tourists, particularly those with means, wished to bring back antique sculptures they had seen to England and so the stately homes of England began to display increasing quantities of classical statuary. This echoed the great collections of the past; most notably the Arundel Marbles from the early-seventeenth century.[4] Eighteenth-century examples survive at Petworth and Newby Hall. These classical statues were often then used to create replicas in lead or artificial stone. An example is given by an anonymous visitor commenting upon a gladiator at Houghton Hall in Norfolk during 1741: 'This gladiator is the original from whence so many have since been taken, and are very common in grand gardens'.[5] This shows that copies were considered acceptable from an early stage. Indeed, copies of various antique statues were present at significant properties such as Kedleston Hall and Wentworth Woodhouse, whilst Holkham Hall is described as being 'filled with casts'.[6]

In England, from the early-eighteenth century, there was commercial manufacture of lead garden statuary and plaster casts after the antique, initially by foreign craftsmen. Also coinciding with the rise in neoclassical taste was innovation and experiment in ceramic technology, leading to the establishment of the Coade stone manufactory and others which are known to have replicated many designs originally created by the London lead-founders 'whose business seems to have declined with the rise of this rival alternative to costly bronze and vulnerable marble'.[7] This was because Coade's designs were intended for use in exactly the same positions as their bronze, lead and plaster equivalents.

By the end of the eighteenth century a transitional style of landscape had developed which was often considered most appropriate for the country house, with ornament being used in the immediate vicinity of the house in the perceived manner of an Italian garden from antiquity. Consequently, balustrading, classical urns, fountains and statuary again rose to prominence. Significant later exponents of this style included Sir Charles Barry and John Claudius Loudon. However, the move away from the Italianate style of garden in the years preceding 1900 undoubtedly led to a corresponding reduction in demand for classically inspired ornaments and the manufacturers of artificial stone suffered as a direct consequence.

The roles performed by garden ornaments in today's landscape are little changed from their roles in earlier eras. In essence, they continue to achieve the same aesthetic and practical requirements as focal points, philosophical statements, personal whims or mere decoration. Symbolically, ornaments defy the natural forces of their surroundings, whether wind, rain, snow or drought. Their visual or symbolic presence remains, whatever the season. As a consequence, artificial stone is an integral part of the history of country house architecture and its associated landscapes.

Chapter I

Clay or Cement?

Artificial stone manufacture can be split into two distinct types: that based on a clay formula such as produced by Coade, Blashfield, Doulton and Pulham; and, that incorporating cement such as produced by Austin & Seeley, Pulham, Chilstone and Haddonstone (Pulham was the only significant manufacturer to have produced both types). In general terms, clay-based manufacturers were predominant in the eighteenth and nineteenth centuries, whilst the greater part of modern artificial stone is cement-based.

The constituent parts of cement-based artificial stone are similar to those of concrete. The oldest concrete discovered dates from around 7000BC in the form of a floor at a site in modern-day Israel, whilst around 2500BC there is some evidence of concrete use in the construction of the pyramids in Egypt.[8] However, it was the Roman discovery of pozzolana cement in the second century BC that led to the development of concrete as we understand it today. In earlier times, the use of the material was principally confined to foundations and wall infill. The first known examples of artificial stone being used, in a position where it was intended to be seen, were lintels cast from sandstone, aggregate and lime-pozzolan cement for the repair of the walls of Carcassonne in South-West France during 1135.[9] In England, the earliest reference I have uncovered relates to Sutton Place in Surrey, where Henry VIII's brewer is recorded as having used 'artificial stone or brick' extensively.[10] The history of modern artificial stone commences in 1722, when Richard Holt took out two patents, having identified a market for such a material.

To understand artificial stone, it is first necessary to consider the natural material it imitates. Arguably, the two most famous building stones in this country are Portland stone and Bath stone. Portland stone is a whitish limestone originating in Dorset. It has been used for major buildings across London, including the Houses of Parliament. Bath stone, warm and yellowish-grey in colour, is quarried near the famous town of Bath and is used to great effect throughout that city. It is these two stones that are most frequently replicated by artificial stone manufacturers. Haddonstone even refer to their designs as being available in Portland and Bath colours.

Clay-based ornamentation is not an obvious alternative to natural stone as 'True terracotta, because of its porosity, is always vulnerable to frost if it is not meticulously prepared and fired'.[11] This is the key reason why the use of terracotta outside in England is unusual whereas it is so suited to the Mediterranean - hence the popularity of artificial stone. Haddonstone offers a terracotta colour to enhance this deceit, thereby providing one solution to the problem.

Whilst cement-based artificial stone can be susceptible to water penetration and frost damage if not properly formulated, Coade stone was a special composition of fired clay which passed through a kiln at very high temperatures, thereby transforming it into a material which is impervious to rain or frost. The clue to Coade is the name by which it was sometimes referred to by the company in its marketing, namely 'Lithodipyra'. This name was created from a bastardisation of the Greek words for 'stone' [litho], 'twice' [di] and 'fired' [pyra].[12] In other words, Coade stone was created by firing the material twice. This was done by taking a fired clay material [possibly Coade stone itself], known as grog, and grinding it up to create a fine powder which was then mixed with unfired ball clay from Devon or Dorset, flint and sand to reduce shrinkage and soda-lime-silica glass to help vitrification.[13] Archives reveal Coade ordered large quantities of between twenty and seventy tons of white clay from Cornwall although, from about 1815, Croggon used a coarser grade.[14] The composition comprised about sixty per cent ball clay, five to ten per cent flint, five to ten per cent fine sand, ten per cent soda-lime-silica glass and ten per cent grog.[15] The resultant mix had a controllable rate of shrinkage through drying and firing far superior to conventional terracotta, which can shrink by twenty per cent. This was particularly important for architectural components where dimensional tolerances have always been critical.

Whilst, in 1799, it was written that the 'arcanum of the composition seems to rest with the proprietors', it is a common misconception that the Coade formula has been lost, although there was undoubtedly secrecy attached to the proportions of the ingredients.[16] The formula itself was never a secret and was even recorded in contemporary publications.[17] Indeed, after Eleanor Coade's death in 1821, her company continued and a number of competitors to Coade evolved with very similar finishes. Contemporaries did, however, record how 'several attempts have been made to establish works on a similar plan, but none has as yet succeeded'.[18] Today, craftsmen such as those at Thomason Cudworth, who have been producing items to their own version of Coade's formula since 1985, can produce similar pieces in very small quantities. However, just as today, companies such as Chilstone and Haddonstone have similar constituents in their mixes, the precise proportions, the mould-making technology, casting and curing techniques are developed independently by different manufacturers over time, with skills developed in-house, making the end products distinctively different. It is rather like the apocryphal tale of a group of Women's Institute

Reproduced by kind permission of City of London, London Metropolitan Archives

View of the River God THAMES 9 feet Figure & 4 SEASONS as placed for Burning, & is to represent Stone at the Lythodipyra at Lambeth

1786 engraving showing the interior of a Coade kiln

members all being given the same cake recipe and every one of them coming up with a cake of different appearance once baked.

To produce a new Coade design from scratch, a master model was first created in ordinary clay at a scale of thirteen inches [330mm] to the foot [305mm], to allow for shrinkage. From the model, plaster moulds were then made. The number of moulds required was determined by the complexity of the piece. The Coade material would then be rolled out into sheets of a uniform three to four inch [75 to 100mm] thickness before being pressed by hand into the plaster mould. This is why, on broken pieces of Coade stone, it is still possible to see the finger marks of the person who made the piece. The object was then allowed to dry, with some moisture being absorbed by the plaster mould, until the shaped clay design resembled leather. By this time it would have contracted sufficiently to shrink away from the plaster mould, making removal from the mould relatively easy. The plaster moulds were expensive to produce and so, after use, they were carefully stored for reuse or adaptation as required. After delaminating the clay from the mould, the various sections of the finished design were assembled whilst undercuts were reworked and joints smoothed. The hollow design was then left to dry again before firing in large muffle kilns which shielded the design from direct flames. The kilns obviously had to be large enough to be able to contain large statues.

A contemporary engraving from 1786, shows the interior of a Coade kiln containing a River God (described as being nine feet tall) together with four seasons statues, a large urn and pedestal, another more ornate pedestal, wall plaques and keystones.[19] A letter from 1790 confirms that 'The composition shrinks about half an inch in a foot in the drying, and about the same in the firing'.[20] However, despite these efforts, shrinkage must have still presented a problem for Haddonstone noted, when replicating a pair of Coade sphinxes in 2005, that the base dimension of one measured 1060mm x 420mm whilst the other measured 1020mm x 397mm, equivalent to a significant variation of 3.75 to 5.5 per cent. There are also surviving contemporary records which describe how one client 'several times refused to accept capitals which had shrunk more than anticipated during their manufacture'.[21]

Coade's expertise included the ability to control and maintain temperature of around 1100 to 1150 degrees centigrade for four days and nights of firing.[22] Undoubtedly, at this stage, the whole production batch depended on the skill of the person known as the fireman, whose experience at achieving and maintaining the correct temperature within the kiln was vital. Once removed from the kiln, Coade stone had a superb creamy surface, slightly shiny in appearance, which retains its crisp, sharp detail far better than its natural equivalents. Apart from shrinkage and delamination of pieces due to poor assembly, the other main problem associated with Coade is believed to have resulted from excessive moisture in the clay body at the time of firing causing deterioration. This may have occurred when work was rushed and atmospheric humidity was high.[23]

Alison Kelly, the renowned Coade expert, believed that 'It was a combination of the factory's meticulous preparation of the raw materials, high temperatures and long firing that distinguished Coade stone from other similar products'.[24] It would be sensible to assume that Coade's methods were based on those established by Holt and Pincot, the latter being her former partner. Alison Kelly correctly states that 'Coade stone is now known to be a ceramic material [...] a form of stonework so resistant to the weather that it is as precise today as when it was originally made'.[25]

Although Coade was labour intensive to produce by today's standards, the contemporary alternative of carved natural stone was significantly more expensive, particularly if multiple units were required. Even a one-off casting in artificial stone could represent a substantial saving. For example, Coade was chosen for the ornate coat of arms in the pediment of the New Bethlehem Hospital [now the Imperial War Museum] in Lambeth at a price of £130 guineas. The client had been quoted £500 for the same design carved in natural stone.[26]

An important subsequent manufacturer of clay-based artificial stone was Blashfield. The basic Blashfield mix comprised clays, principally from Dorset, Devon and later Stamford, with silica and other fusible materials. Through Blashfield's own writings, we know far more about his manufacturing methods than any other company, making the following account invaluable:

The plaster moulds should be tolerably dry (that is, the water used in mixing the plaster, with which they are made, should have partially evaporated) before they are used. For terra cotta work, sheets of clay are beaten on a bench to a consistency of painter's putty, and pressed by hand into these moulds. According to the magnitude of the work and the weight it may have to sustain, the thickness of the clay is determined and arranged, and here consists a part of the art it would be impossible to describe, and which requires years of experience in such matters to produce great works, and fire them with certainty of success.

After the clay has been allowed to dry a little in the plaster mould, the latter is removed, and a clay moulded article is exhibited – more properly speaking, a clay casting or impression is exhibited, but moulding is the potter's term for such work. Upon this clay article the joints and seams of the mould are seen as upon a plaster cast, and the same amount of care and skill is required for their removal. In all works of art this is done by a skilled workman or artist, who at the same time carefully goes over the work, and undercuts such parts as are necessary, and repairs any defects which appear on the surface of the impression. The work is then left to dry gradually, and lest it should become twisted it must be carefully watched, and in the case of statues props and supports will be required. The drying of large and valuable works, their subsequent removal to the kiln and the process of burning will cause much anxiety to the manufacturer. One mistake or slight accident may totally destroy an original work of several hundred pounds' value.

After the moulded article has become sufficiently dry for baking, it is conveyed to a kiln, and requires careful handling, as it is very fragile and easily chipped; and when the kiln is filled with articles, a slow fire is at first made, and gradually quickened; the articles are baked and become terra cotta. The heat should be of sufficient intensity to blend and partially vitrify the materials of which the mass is composed without melting or distorting the ware. As soon as this temperature is

obtained, the firing is stopped, and all apertures closed, to prevent the admission
of cold air. When the kiln has cooled, the articles are withdrawn, and unless
required to be painted and glazed, are finished.[27]

Whilst artificial stone based on Portland cement is a relatively recent innovation, man has been searching for stone substitutes for several thousand years. The chief breakthrough came with the discovery by James Parker of a natural cement produced from nodules found in clay on the Isle of Sheppey. Ground down and heated in a kiln, these nodules created a powder, which formed the basis for what became known as 'Roman Cement'. Parker took out a patent in 1796. When this expired in 1810, competitors rapidly entered the marketplace with more that forty different formulations available by 1819. In 1830, however, an alternative made from chalk and a blue clay from the Medway was introduced and quickly gained favour as 'Portland Cement'. This laid the foundations for the cement industry in this country.[28] By 1863, Portland cement was deemed to be 'quite common cast in ornaments'.[29]

The modern definition of cast stone in the British Standards is 'any material manufactured with aggregate and cementitious binder, intended to resemble in appearance, and which may be used in a similar way to, natural stone'.[30] The Architectural Cladding Association (ACA) identifies that there are 'two very different methods of manufacturing reconstructed stone, which produce two materials with different properties. These are known as wet-cast reconstructed stone and semi-dry reconstructed stone'.[31]

The ACA provides relatively succinct descriptions of the two cement-based methods. Wet-cast reconstructed stone 'is a plastic mix of aggregates, cement and sometimes pigment, and water, which can be poured into a mould. It is compacted by vibration. Wet-cast reconstructed stone has a high strength and a low absorption rate'.[32] Conversely, the semi-dry equivalent, is also

known as the "moist earth" mix method. As the name implies, the material has a low water content and has the same texture as moist earth when freshly mixed. It is consolidated in the mould by ramming or tamping. Semi-dry reconstructed stone has a surface texture and colour closely resembling those of some natural stones. It has relatively lower strength and higher porosity compared to wet-cast, and can only be manufactured in fairly small unit sizes. [33]

The performance of modern cast stone can, however, be impressive. For example: 'Haddonstone has a proven ability to withstand exposure to saltwater and wind off the North Sea, as the material has passed strenuous salt crystallisation and water absorption tests conducted by the highly respected BRE laboratories'.[34]

Early cement-based artificial stone is believed to have been composed of a mix of Portland cement and fine aggregates cast into plaster moulds. Unfortunately, no contemporary accounts exist for the production of cement-based artificial stone designs from the likes of Austin & Seeley and Pulham, although it has been speculated that designs would have been cast in large components into a flexible compound held rigid by plaster.[35] Consequently, it is best to look in detail at the production process undertaken by Haddonstone, the current leading company in this field, and assume that a more primitive version would have been the method undertaken by its illustrious forebears.

At Haddonstone, specialist contracts staff provide budget prices or quotations for each individual product or project, often accompanied by detailed drawings. The saving in cost over a carved stone equivalent will largely depend on the amount of repetition involved, although notable past projects such as the Lyceum Theatre in Sheffield in 1992, have proved that artificial stone can be more economical than carved stone even when significant numbers of unique moulds are required. Increasingly, architects do not provide much more than schematic drawings of façades, leaving much of the detailed drawing work to the manufacturing company. Haddonstone currently employs a contracts manager, an assistant contracts manager, four estimators, a secretary and two architectural sales personnel. An export manager and export estimator provide for overseas clients. Obviously, if Haddonstone is specified on an architect's drawings or in a bill of materials, then this is much to the company's advantage. This is why Haddonstone expends significant sums on marketing via journal advertising, exhibitions, printed catalogues and electronic mediums including the company website, which contains significant information on the company's products as well as methods of construction and CAD drawings.

Once the client has approved drawings, and a deposit has been received, a mould is required before production can commence. Obviously, if the order is for a standard design, then production can commence as soon as a colour has been agreed. All Haddonstone products are currently available in three standard colours: Portland and Bath to closely match the carved equivalent, as well as terracotta. Colour matching is also possible, principally for restoration projects.

If the design is relatively simple, a window cill or coping stone, for example, then the mould will be made of wood in the company's own wood shop. One of eleven skilled carpenters will interpret the mould drawings created by the contracts department to produce a precise mould, which is the exact reverse of the shape ultimately required. If different lengths of the same profile stone are required then the larger size will be produced and blocking pieces provided so that many different lengths can be economically manufactured from the same basic mould. Timber moulds have a comparatively limited life when compared to their fibreglass equivalents. However, the speed with which timber moulds can be produced, combined with their relatively low cost, normally makes this type of mould more economical for the client.

The production of a fibreglass, rubber-lined mould in the company's studio is much more time-consuming than timber mould manufacture and is only undertaken if the design is complex or if there are likely to be numerous castings over time, perhaps because the design is for an item to be added to the standard range. The work in this area is one of the most highly skilled within Haddonstone, benefiting greatly from artistic and practical skills. A staff of six is currently employed in Haddonstone's studio.

Haddonstone's studio, showing the carving of a plaster model

Before a mould can be made, it is first necessary to have a model. This can come from a variety of sources: it could be created by the neighbouring wood shop; it could have been carved from scratch by either a freelance sculptor or in-house craftsman, normally in plaster, either replicating an antique piece for a restoration project or afresh for a new design; it could be a pristine antique piece of stone, perhaps even a design by Coade, Blashfield or Doulton; or it could be a damaged original requiring partial or extensive restoration before mould-making can commence.

Once the master model has been created, the mould-making can begin. This is done by rolling clay to a set thickness and covering the entire model. Over this a fibreglass case is formed. As this case will be completely inflexible, it has to be designed in such a way as to allow its later removal. For this reason, some fibreglass cases can comprise more than ten sections.

Then the fibreglass case is removed, the model extricated and all traces of clay removed. The fibreglass case is then reassembled around the model, there now being a void where the clay had previously been. Into that void is poured a specially developed rubber which has enough fluidity to fill every cavity whilst avoiding any air bubbles which would be seen in the finished design. After the rubber has set, the fibreglass case is, once again, removed and the model extricated for storage. When the fibreglass and rubber case is reassembled, the void now left in the centre is the precise shape and size of the finished design. Particular care is taken to ensure that any seam is in a position where it is least noticeable. The seam is often the only way a casual observer can ultimately tell that the piece has been cast rather than carved. Whether wooden or fibreglass, without a first-class mould it is impossible to create a first-class product. Unlike its terracotta equivalent, the cement-based manufacturing process needs to make no allowance for shrinkage.

Over time, and with experience, each artificial stone manufacturer will inevitably develop its own mix, incorporating many ingredients, which remain closely guarded secrets; in much the same way as the Coade factory guarded their formulae two centuries before. At Haddonstone, the principal materials are limestone, white cement, sand and a small quantity of water. This produces the Portland colour with other colours requiring the addition of pigment into the mix. There are other key ingredients including plasticisers to improve workability and aid compaction as well as waterproofers. To ensure complete control of the production process, every single batch of raw material delivered to the Haddonstone manufactory is quality checked, before it is used, to ensure it meets the company's precise specifications. The constituents of the mix are stored in high-tonnage silos adjacent to the production area, before being mixed in small quantities via computer controlled batching equipment and taken to a workstation. At this stage, the semi-dry mix has the feel of damp sand or earth.

The main factory floor is divided into sections for garden ornaments, architectural designs, balustrading and special, otherwise known as custom-made, designs. By creating sections, operatives become specialists in their field, thereby reducing the possibility of seconds or reject quality stone being produced. The stone is gradually packed into the mould using a number of ingeniously crafted tools. Whilst this is normally done by hand, some moulds can be packed using pneumatic hand rammers. Care has to be taken to ensure that only appropriate quantities of the mix are compacted at a time, otherwise a layering effect will be seen on the finished design. Once packed, the stone is left in the mould until the next working day. This is the same process whether the mould is of wood or fibreglass.

The process of delaminating or stripping is probably the most visually rewarding of the entire production process, particularly for a fibreglass mould. Here, each bolt holding the fibreglass case together is removed and the fibreglass case stripped away, leaving the rubber around the stone. The rubber is then carefully peeled away to reveal the stone design in all its glory. No finishing is required as the quality of mould manufacture ensures that the design is perfect. It is at this stage that the product is moved onto a pallet and the first of many quality control checks is undertaken and the product is given a bar code label, which will remain with it until delivery to the customer.

The stone is now strong enough to be transported outside the production area. Like other companies in the industry, Haddonstone originally relied on the vagaries of the English climate to ensure that the stone cured correctly. However, the effects of temperature, precipitation and wind made this a very inexact science. For this reason, the company developed a controlled-curing environment before introducing a vapour curing system in 1999 that gives the stone the equivalent of fourteen days strength overnight. A recent visitor noted how this system functions: 'A gas burner heats an insulated chamber to forty degrees centigrade and steam is injected to reach one hundred per cent humidity. This forces moisture into the stone, accelerating the hydration of the cement and carbonation which bonds the aggregate particles together'.[36] Not only does vapour curing give the company a guaranteed curing system, it also reduces lead times and storage problems. The dry-cast stone now has a surface texture remarkably similar to natural Portland stone; 'Quality cast stone looks so much like natural stone that it is hard to tell the difference even when touching it'.[37]

Once vapour cured, the product is moved to its designated position in the storage yard, the bar code being swiped to ensure that the precise location of each design is known, making 'picking' for delivery very straightforward. Although some customers opt to collect their orders, most rely on Haddonstone's own transport fleet, the majority of which include a demountable forklift to aid off-loading on site. Export orders are dispatched by container or in specially constructed wooden crates. A similar operation to Haddonstone's manufactory at Brixworth in Northamptonshire exists at the company's satellite production facilities as well as at the company's US manufactory, which opened at Pueblo in Colorado during 1996. Haddonstone's Northamptonshire production facilities currently employ eighty-two personnel with an additional thirty staff at the company's East Haddon head office. Forty-four personnel are employed by Haddonstone (USA) Ltd in Pueblo, Colorado, plus seven at the company's office and warehouse in Bellmawr, New Jersey.

In the UK and USA, Haddonstone also manufactures by a wet-cast process, which it calls Haddon-TecStone or TecStone. Here, the mix is poured into the mould. This process gives a finish, once acid etched, much more akin to Coade stone and is ideal for larger products, complex statuary often produced in component form and contemporary designs where clients prefer a surface finish which does not weather quickly. Most recently, Haddonstone has developed an artificial stone reinforced with glass fibres, which it calls TecLite. Products made by this process have thinner walls and are consequently lighter.

Chapter II

Coade's Pre-eminence

A spirit of technological innovation gained momentum as the eighteenth century progressed culminating in a period normally now known as the Industrial Revolution. The need for increased production, driven by an expanding population and Empire, saw advances in many fields, including building materials.

Most garden historians agree that 'The earliest substitute for stone in the production of sculptured figures and monuments was Coade ware, which was an artificial stone whose manufacture and precise composition is not known, as it was naturally a secret jealously guarded by the factory'.[38] However, this significantly oversimplifies the story. Sir William Chambers, for example, instructed lead statues to be painted with stone dust at Blenheim.

Coade stone was an artificial stone manufactured by Mrs Eleanor Coade from 1769, when she set up a manufactory in Lambeth. However, she was definitely not the first to create artificial stone. At least three others came before: Richard Holt, Batty Langley and Daniel Pincot. Coade can, however, still be considered one of the first for, whilst thirty patents for 'making artificial stone' are listed for the period 1722 to 1848, only three were from before 1800.[39]

Holt

Richard Holt took out two patents for making artificial stone in 1722, although they were so deliberately vague that their precise composition cannot now be determined, being described as a 'Compound Liquid Metall [...] by which Artificiall Stone and Marble is made by casting or running the Metall into Moulds [...] for House Work and Garden Ornaments'.[40] Interestingly, the use of the word 'metall' is not as contrary as is generally asserted by modern artificial stone historians, a sixteenth century definition being 'Material, matter, substance; *esp.* earthy matter' whilst in the eighteenth century it was in use as a term for 'Hardened clay'.[41] In 1730, after about five or six years of production, Holt published *A Short Treatise of Artificial Stone*.[42] It is a fascinating document, which dismisses Portland stone as an uncertain material, Bath stone as a treacherous one and which claims that the ancients mistrusted natural stone and so created a superior artificial stone whose qualities far exceeded its natural equivalents. He even contends that Stonehenge and the Egyptian Pyramids must have been made of this composition. Although Holt's treatise can easily be dismissed as the ramblings of a madman, his convictions as to the superiority of his artificial stone were based on much research, his travels in search of ancient formulae taking him 'into Asia and African Turkey'.[43]

Holt describes his artificial stone as follows: 'my SECRET COMPOSITION [...] consists of such Incredients, as are, by a strong Heat of Fire, reduc'd to the state of Fluidity; melted and run down into *a most compact Solid Mass*, according to the Shape and Dimensions of the given Model. I say, my COMPOSITION consists of such *ingredients*, as (when hot) have a Natural Tendancy to *Fluidity* and *Vitrification*; and (when cold) consolidate into the *hardest Stone* [...] by the means of a few *Simple Ingredients*, I am able to run down *my Clays*, or even the *hardest Rock* in *England*, and cast them in the assign'd *Moulds*, as fast as the *Lead-Men* do their most *Fluid Metal*'.[44] Although very confident of the capabilities of his own material, he was obviously very frustrated by the attempts of others to obtain the secrets of his methods by 'Villainous' means, with his workmen being bribed and otherwise cajoled into revealing this information.[45] The chief perpetrator of this was Batty Langley who threatened to set up in opposition unless he was given a share of Holt's business, believing that he could circumnavigate Holt's patent.[46] As Langley did set up in opposition one can only assume that Holt refused to acquiesce to this blackmail. Until that time, Holt appears to have had the field to himself.

Sadly, because of his understandably cautious, perhaps deliberately vague, description of his techniques, very little information regarding Holt's manufacturing process survives, although one contemporary account reports that he produced a 'good round catalogue […including…] Columns, Pedestals, Entablatures, Cornices, Pediments, Ballustrades, Statues, Rusticks, Fascias, Coppings of Walls and Chimney Pieces, Hearthstones, Architraves, Fronticepieces of Doors, Windows, Alcoves and Grottos, Cascades, Obelisques, Arches, Piazzas, Key-Stones, Stops, Pavements, Urns, Balls […] Tomb-Stones, Monuments, Sundials, Crests for Doors, Gates and Gateways, Statuary of all Sorts […] of a beautiful White or Freestone Colour'.[47] It is believed that Holt's products were created from a ceramic material, which required heating or firing.[48] In appearance, his designs were described by a contemporary as being 'all covered on one side with an earthen ware, white glaze'.[49] Holt ran his business in Lambeth, in the vicinity but not at the same location where the Coade factory would ultimately become established. Lambeth, which features so strongly in the history of artificial stone production, had been an important centre for pottery production since the sixteenth century, possibly before.[50]

Holt's key commissions included Orleans House in Twickenham and Chiswick House.[51] Unfortunately, Holt's dates of birth and death are unknown although his business apparently died with his passing.[52] By the time Coade had appeared on the scene, Holt's business is described as having 'fallen into very low circumstances'.[53] It has even been speculated that Holt, suffering from ill health, spent a period of convalescence at Lyme Regis where he met the Coades whilst they were conducting early experiments into artificial stone production using local clay, subsequently selling his moulds and factory to the Coades.[54] Alison Kelly has found no evidence to support these suggestions.[55] However, as Holt's designs have been described as showing 'neither taste in the designs, nor neatness in their execution', not deficiencies normally associated with Coade stone, a direct connection between Holt and the Coades would seem very unlikely.[56] As Holt's formula is now known to have included lead ore, which Coade stone did not, this also seems to prove that Coade's formula was not taken from Holt, or at least not directly.[57]

Langley

Batty Langley (1696-1751), who lived variously in Twickenham, Westminster and

Soho, is best known as the prolific author of architectural and landscaping titles aimed at keeping builders and their patrons abreast of the latest trends. Langley has been described as 'not intellectually inclined, nor given to original concepts either in gardening or in architecture. He was however extremely alert to new ideas and fashions'.[58]

Langley may well have turned to artificial stone owing to his comparative failure as an architect, spurred on by the need to support a wife and fourteen children![59] Intriguingly, as a fervent freemason, this change of career would appear to have gone against his colleagues' interests. However, this would probably not have overly concerned Langley who appears to have been something of a rogue, flitting from one business venture to the next, being described by Holt as 'a certain pretending Architect, a meddling busy Man […] full of new Fangles, that has already deserted several Trades'.[60] He is even described by George Vertue in 1731 as 'a bold faced undertaker' who had 'A New invention of casting in stone or a hard composition […] made near Lambeth'.[61] In order to judge one person's opinion of another, one normally has to 'read between the lines' when reading eighteenth-century documents, making these statements all the more damning. However, Horace Walpole is far more generous, ignoring Holt's contribution, yet stating that Langley 'invented an artificial stone, of which he made figures: an art lately brought to great perfection'.[62] He is also described as having 'manufactured an artificial stone, of which he made statues, busts and architectural ornaments'.[63] Langley's business was established in Southwark.[64]

After the demise of Holt and Langley, there is no evidence to suggest that artificial stone was produced again until the 1760s.[65]

Pincot

In 1766 John Gwynn argued that, as brick was too mean and stone so expensive for public buildings, then encouragement should 'be given to some ingenious person to find out a stucco or composition resembling stone […] at a very easy expense'.[66]

Months later, on 10 February 1767, Daniel Pincot (?-1797) announced that he had 'set up a Manufacturer of Artificial Stone […] making all sorts of rich carved ornament used in Buildings'.[67] This is a key date as it confirms that Pincot was manufacturing before Coade. Unlike Holt, Pincot never claimed to have invented the process, and he did not take out any patent. Indeed, he seems to have had more than one recipe.[68] However, as his Goldstone Square premises were later referred to as being the 'original' artificial stone works, this does suggest the process was uniquely developed by Pincot.[69] Pincot's manufactory was located at Goldstone Square in Whitechapel with a warehouse at 18 Long Acre.[70] Pincot was showing examples of his work at the Free Society of Artists' Exhibition in 1767.[71]

Late in 1767 Pincot moved his manufactory to Narrow Wall, Lambeth, where Eleanor Coade joined him, although their business relationship did not last long.[72] Gunnis states that 'There were other manufactures of artificial stone in London before Mrs. Coade', citing as proof a sale of a hundred items of artificial stone at Christie's in December 1767.[73] This sale was actually of Pincot's wares. A further sale by Christie occurred in June 1771. The 1767 date coincides with a time just prior to Coade's arrival on the scene when Pincot was experiencing business difficulties and consequently needed a new partner. Meanwhile, 1771 coincides with the year he acrimoniously parted from Coade and could well have had some of his original stock remaining in his name, which needed to be sold quickly. His influence lived on through one of Coade's most famous models, the Borghese Vase, which Pincot exhibited in 1769, with examples being sold in his name to Stourhead in 1770 and Kedleston in 1771.[74]

What happened to Pincot after his split from Coade is not recorded although, with his knowledge, he would surely have remained involved within the industry in some way. However, if he did set up in business again, like others, he must have been unsuccessful as, in 1784, it is noted that 'there have been several other Manufactories passing under the same denomination' which have been extinct for some years.[75]

In 1770 Pincot published *An Essay on the Origin, Nature, Uses, and Properties, of Artificial Stone*, a fascinating text in which he attempts to trace the history of artificial stone back to Noah, whilst also including accounts of the open hostility to artificial stone from contemporary stonemasons. His essay has correctly been described as an 'eccentric, disjointed history'.[76]

Another manufacturer operating in Lambeth prior to Coade's existence was The London Pottery of James Stiff & Sons, which was established in 1751 and expanded from 1840.[77] Products included 'garden vases, pedestals, chimney-tops, window arches, string-courses, &c'.[78]

Coade

Eleanor Coade (1733-1821) was born in Devon, the daughter of a wool merchant. Following the bankruptcy of her father, William, in 1759 the family moved to

Reproduced by kind permission of City of London, London Metropolitan Archives

Exterior view of Coade's Lambeth factory in the 1790s

London. Eleanor went into business as a linen draper in the mid-1760s, no doubt gaining valuable business experience. In 1769 Eleanor's father died and she joined Daniel Pincot's artificial stone business at King's Arms Stairs, Narrow Wall, Lambeth – close to the location of the Royal Festival Hall today. As a consequence, it is currently assumed that her father's influence on the business was slight, if at all. However, this does not explain why, as late as 1787, a monument to Edward Wortley Montague in Westminster Abbey Cloisters bears the signature 'E. and W. Coade'.[79] It is currently impossible to shed any further light on this intriguing attribution. Quite where the money came from for this new venture is unclear, although it has been speculated that, as the Coade family were Dissenters or nonconformists, who have a tradition of helping each other, then investment may have come from other Dissenters [Pincot was also a Dissenter] or from Eleanor's extended family.[80] How Eleanor decided to embark on this enterprise is also unclear, although china clay can be found in Dorset from where the Coade family originated.[81] Pincot must have had the practical knowledge of artificial stone production that Eleanor lacked, there being no record of her family having previously been involved with any form of terracotta production.[82] However, in 1771, Eleanor sacked Pincot for representing himself as the sole proprietor of the factory. Eleanor placed announcements in the *Daily Advertiser*, effectively dissolving the partnership and ejecting Pincot from the premises. Just two weeks later, John Bacon had been appointed as the Superintendent of the Manufactory.[83] This episode clearly shows Eleanor's firm business mind.

John Bacon (1740-1799) had been apprenticed at Nicholas Crispe's porcelain factory in Vauxhall, with workshops in Bow and Lambeth. He remained with Crispe until 1764 when he began designing for the ceramic and metalwork industries, one of his clients being Daniel Pincot. Other, far more illustrious clients included Sir William Chambers, Lewis Vulliamy and Josiah Wedgwood. Largely self-taught, Bacon was very highly regarded as an artist, receiving the Royal Academy's first ever gold medal for sculpture in 1769, before becoming an associate of the Academy a year later. In 1771 he established a sculpture workshop in Marylebone, employing twenty assistants.[84] Indeed, one wonders whether Pincot's departure from Coade was engineered by Eleanor so as to make way for this well-connected and accomplished

Coade's factory yard in the 1790s, featuring the famous River God statue

artist who seemed to have possessed a business mind as shrewd as her own. The fact that Bacon was also a Dissenter would have helped cement their bond, as Bacon remained with Coade for the rest of his life; he was, in effect, both chief designer and manager. He became a Royal Academician in 1778, an appointment that recognised his talent and was undoubtedly exploited by Coade to prove the high design integrity of the firm. In one obituary, it is even stated that, during Bacon's apprenticeship at Crispe's, 'he formed a design of making statues in artificial stone, which he afterwards perfected. The manufactory now carried on at Lambeth by Mrs. Coade originated with him'.[85] As recently as 1966, *The Times* reported that 'The material, a kind of terra-cotta, is believed by some to have been invented by the elder John Bacon, the sculptor. It began to be developed by Mrs. Eleanor Coade'.[86] These previously unreported statements, if true, would have a significant impact on

Coade's reputation.

The London Building Act of 1774 banned wooden porches and decorations in order to prevent fire. Coming just three years after she took sole control of the business, this undoubtedly gave Eleanor Coade the opportunity to expand into a new market by supplying designs including door surrounds and keystones. Likewise, Coade always attempted to keep pace with fashion, creating, for example, designs in a Greek style when that became popular, as well as colossal Egyptian figures when Egyptian art became fashionable.

Although Eleanor Coade copied many antique originals such as the Borghese and Medici vases, which were her longest selling models, she was shrewd enough to engage a series of first class modellers as well as architects, whilst also cultivating a high level of clientele, up to and including the King. The Coade business was indeed fortunate that it produced work that appealed to both King George III as well as his son, later George IV, as most designers who appealed to the father were despised by the son, and vice versa! Eleanor Coade had a royal appointment to George III and to the Prince of Wales as both Prince Regent and, later, George IV.[87] As well as John Bacon, Eleanor also employed at least four other Royal Academicians: Thomas Banks, John Flaxman, John Charles Felix Rossi and Benjamin West.[88] She also worked with all the leading architects of her day, including Robert Adam, Sir William Chambers, John Nash, Sir John Soane and both James and Samuel Wyatt.[89] Indeed, an impressive total of 138 architects have been identified as users of Coade stone.[90]

The products themselves were competitively priced, finely detailed, high-grade and durable. Remarkably, within ten years of the company's formation, Coade was able to produce an illustrated catalogue of more than 250 items.[91] The 1784 Catalogue included 'Statues, Busts, Vases, Pedestals, Capitals, Frizes, Fascias, Pannels and Tablets, Medallions, Pateras for Elevations, Coats of Arms, Imposts, Key-Stones, Architraves, Rustics, Pinnacles, Balusters, Balls and Feet, Chimney Tops, Piers, Consoles, Sepulchral Ornaments, Chimney-Pieces, Pieces of Furniture,

Ornaments and Wood Chimney Pieces with Stone Ornaments'.[92] As with any commercial operation, whether in the eighteenth or twenty-first centuries, designs were produced in whatever style was demanded by the patrons. As a consequence, the manufacturer is susceptible to changes in fashion as well as the caprices of the client, although Eleanor Coade could 'satisfy customers who had a real knowledge of classical sculpture'.[93] Just as Haddonstone has an impressive library today, Coade had access to numerous primary and secondary classical works, including plaster casts, volumes from the Capitoline Museums in Rome and the works of Charles Tatham.[94] From whatever source they came, Coade's designs undoubtedly display the same reverence for the classical past as inspired the whole neo-classical movement.

Coade stone was generally considered 'inexpensive' although the most expensive item in her 1784 catalogue, the famous River God, was priced at one hundred guineas. By contrast, an Ionic capital was just thirteen shillings.[95] When Horace Walpole queried the price of £150 for two gate piers at his Strawberry Hill residence in Twickenham, he asked Sir William Chambers to act for him. A thorough examination of the work involved concluded that the price would have been fairer at just under £152, exclusive of profit.[96] In reality, the Strawberry Hill controversy must have been very useful to Eleanor Coade as it showed her prices were fair and that she was scrupulously honest and, even though Walpole never ordered from Coade again, Chambers became a regular specifier of her wares. As a consequence of her competitive pricing strategy, the production by the Lambeth factory was vast. The 1784 catalogue incorporated numerous architectural elements, reflecting the fact that that side of the business had developed so that the company was so much more than a producer of garden ornaments.[97]

In 1786, Coade's Lambeth works were noted as 'very extensive, being calculated to answer every purpose of stone carving', whilst her statues were said to be 'master-pieces of art', the prices were 'much below the price of stone, and in many particulars considerably cheaper than wood', concluding that 'This infant manufactory certainly deserves some distinguishing encouragement'.[98] In 1799, Coade's works are described as being 'executed with more delicacy and sharpness than is to be found in the best sculptures'.[99]

Eleanor Coade remained unmarried, yet is often given the courtesy title of 'Mrs' as was the custom for unmarried women in business at the time. She may have been a talented modeller in her own right as exhibits appear in her name at the Society of Artists between 1773 and 1780. However, as the Georgian understanding of artistic ownership and copyright were different from ours today, she may have simply laid claim to these pieces, as they were the products manufactured by her firm.[100] Indeed, this hypothesis is supported by the actions of Eleanor Coade herself, as she later attributed some of these works to John Bacon.[101] However, at least half of the pieces exhibited are now believed to be of Eleanor's own creation.[102]

The Eleanor Coade who ran the business has often been confused with her mother of the same name, in part because the unmarried daughter was most frequently referred to as 'Mrs. Coade'. However, it is now held that it was the daughter who was the driving force behind the business.[103] Despite this, her mother is believed to have had a conservative or restraining influence on the company until her death in 1796.[104] Indeed, it was only after her mother's passing that greater efforts were made to attract increasing business, the opening of Coade's Gallery in 1799 being the most obvious consequence. The gallery handbook includes a list of hundreds of Coade commissions from 1769 to 1799 and, although not comprehensive, does indicate the scale of Coade's achievements.

Coade stone's 'versatility allowed it to be used for all architectural details, commemorative and funerary monuments, fonts, statues, busts, coats of arms, chimney-pieces, garden ornaments, and furniture. Most is neo-classical, but there were also Gothic commissions'.[105] Amongst the countless examples of Coade stone at country houses are the River God at Ham House in Surrey, the Triton Fountain at Petworth in West Sussex, the Borghese vase at Wrest Park in Bedfordshire and the Umbrello at Great Saxham Hall in Suffolk.[106] Also the Medici vase located at Kew.[107] The Medici and Borghese vases were amongst the company's longest selling

Coade's etching of the Borghese vase

designs.[108] The Borghese vase is known to have been first produced by Coade in 1771 and was still in production until at least 1827.[109] Commissions were supplied across the British Isles and around the world including Brazil, Canada, the Caribbean, Ireland, the Netherlands, Poland, Russia, South Africa and the United States of America.[110] The aforementioned Umbrello at Great Saxham is 'one of the very few garden buildings constructed of Coade stone' and its survival into the twenty-first century material is largely due to the material's resistance to damp and frost.[111] Another landscape structure reliably attributed to Coade is the Gothic Seat at Ascot Place in Berkshire.[112]

Interestingly, although Coade was used by all the great architects of that period, the most extensive use was normally reserved for secondary buildings or landscapes. Examples are the Orangery at Burton Constable in Yorkshire, the Island Temple at Croome Park in Worcestershire, the stable block at Gosford House in East Lothian, the gateway lodges at Langley Park in Norfolk, garden ornaments for the Royal Lodge at Windsor, the Buckingham Lodges at Stowe, the ornamental gateway and screens at Easton Neston in Northamptonshire, the Gothic summerhouse at Brightling Park in Sussex, the exotic Indian-style folly at Sezincote in Gloucestershire, the River God statue and Pineapple finials at Ham House in Surrey and the magnificent fountain at Petworth in Sussex. Indeed, it has been noted that the great landowners of England, Scotland and Ireland 'were mostly interested in sculptures and garden ornaments'.[113]

There are exceptions, where Coade stone has been used in an architectural context, such as Heaton Hall in Manchester, where James Wyatt used monumental Coade stone columns on the façade, Pitzhanger Manor in London, where Soane used Ionic columns surmounted by caryatids on his own house and a portico in front of the house at Shugborough in Staffordshire. Hans van Lemmen states that Coade 'produced all kinds of architectural ornaments for the decoration of town and country houses. It could be in the form of statues, capitals for columns, ornamental friezes, and garden furniture, but occasionally whole structures like small summerhouses or ornamental archways were made of Coade stone'.[114] Even 'where large new houses were being built Coade's part in construction was more or less limited'.[115] However, it has been noted that some Coade architectural designs were stamped on the edge of the piece and so the evidence would be concealed once built.[116] This would make attribution virtually impossible, potentially meaning that Coade was more extensively used than is currently recognised. In general terms, Coade seems to have been used where significant savings could be made when high levels of ornamentation were required on subsidiary structures. Indeed, for all its undoubted qualities, it would not appear that Coade was the material of choice when it came to the main house. As a consequence, one can only assume that there remained a prejudice against the use of this exquisite material, which, paradoxically, has survived far better than its natural counterparts. This can result in significant restoration costs today, when the deteriorating carved stone requires complete or partial replacement.

Eleanor Coade's death in 1821 warranted an obituary in the *Gentleman's Magazine,* which credited her as 'sole inventor and proprietor of an art which deserves considerable notice. In 1769 a burnt artificial stone manufactory was erected by Mrs Coade […] This manufactory has been carried on from that time to the present on a very extensive scale, being calculated to answer every purpose of stone carving, having a property peculiar to itself of resisting the frost and consequently of retaining that sharpness in which it excels every kind of stone sculpture and even equals marble itself'.[117]

Coade was 'Probably one of the most successful synthetic building materials ever invented', the boom in the construction or remodelling of country houses during the eighteenth century, partly in response to the classical influences of the Grand Tour, undoubtedly creating a significant market for Coade stone as well as the company's rivals who proliferated in the early-nineteenth century.[118] Coade led its market, but inadvertently encouraged the rise of fellow participants. After Coade's closure, Blanchard and Blashfield, along with Austin & Seeley, successfully filled the void. Whilst it has recently been stated that Coade's decline may have been 'due to the parallel rediscovery of concrete', this is nonsense, as it ignores the tremendous commercial success of those that followed Coade.[119]

Sealy

John Sealy (1749-1813) was a cousin of Eleanor Coade on her father's side of the family. He worked for the company from the early 1790s before becoming a partner in the business in 1799, which then became known as Coade & Sealy. A showroom was then opened at the Lambeth end of Westminster Bridge, a special pamphlet being produced to mark the occasion.[120] Sealy was both an able manager and an accomplished clay modeller.[121] The key sculptor during this period following Bacon's passing appears to have been Joseph Panzetta (fl. 1789-1830) whilst Thomas Dubbin was foreman of the works and also visited architects and patrons.[122] Sealy died in 1813 whilst in America promoting Coade stone and both he and his wife are buried at Lambeth, where a large Coade stone monument covers the family vault in the churchyard.[123] John Davies, in his 2008 'Artificial Stone' lecture, hypothesised about the likely family connection between John Sealy of Coade & Sealy and John Seeley of Austin & Seeley.

Croggon

William Croggon (c1777-1835) was appointed manager in 1813 following the death of John Sealy. The firm reverted to the Coade name and continued to flourish, although Eleanor never made Croggon a partner. Croggon was in some way related to Eleanor Coade's aunt and was, therefore, a distant cousin.[124] He became responsible for the company in Eleanor Coade's latter years and by 1814 she was taking no active part in the business.[125] On Coade's death in 1821, Croggon was disappointed to find that he had not been left the business and so was forced to purchase the company from Eleanor Coade's heirs. He then ran the business in his own name from the same premises in Lambeth.

As a consequence, historians of artificial stone are fortunate that Croggon's Day Book, Order Book and Letter Book survive in the National Archives.[126] Originally discovered in the late 1960s, having been deposited as part of a Chancery case during Croggon's difficult settlement with Eleanor Coade's heirs, these documents contain the only substantial archive relating to artificial stone, apart from records held informally by current manufacturers such as Haddonstone. They relate principally to the period from 1813 to 1821 and are the most important primary source material relating to Coade still extant. The archive material covers the final years of Eleanor Coade's life, casting a spotlight on the company's customers, orders and costs. John Ruch was the first person to properly study this material.[127]

The years 1816 to 1820 saw a period of expansion for the firm, although increasing costs and general economic instability had seen prices rise by about ten per cent during the 1810s.[128] At around this time, Croggon even set up a north London branch on Palace Row in New Road, now Euston Road.[129] Production levels were impressive, and include commissions between 1826 and 1828 for Buckingham Palace: six vases to the terrace; seven statues, principally for the Grand Entrance; reliefs for the west front; and capitals, pillars and trophies for the Quadrangle.[130] The labour force rose from fifteen to about twenty-two between 1813 and 1821.[131] Exports are recorded as far afield as Brazil, Canada, Gibraltar, India, South Africa, Sri Lanka and the West Indies.[132] From 1818, Croggon diversified into the production of imitation marble called scagliola, that became an important and lucrative part of the business.[133]

Despite all this success, in 1833 Croggon was declared bankrupt.[134] It has been suggested that this was possibly because of an unpaid debt from the Duke of York.[135] Croggon's youngest son, Thomas John Croggon (1813-84), refounded his father's business but the firm's fortunes soon waned, the premises being leased out in 1837.[136] The last significant dated piece of Coade to have been found is on the large

Coade's magnificent lion from the Lion Brewery, now standing outside London's County Hall

lion from the former Lion Brewery, inscribed 24 May 1837.[137] The famous lion now stands outside London's County Hall. Pieces have been found with dates as late as 1840 with the moulds and some remaining production being sold in 1843.[138] It may have been the development of cement-based artificial stone, requiring far less hand finishing and which Croggon was unable to compete against, or it may simply have been a more routine business problem such as a bad debt, which ultimately brought about the fall of the company. Why the company actually failed will probably remain unknown even though it is somewhat surprising considering the success of competitors who filled the void left by the once dominant Coade business. In about 1840, many of the moulds and models were sold by auction to Blashfield and Blanchard.[139]

Chapter III

The Nineteenth-century Followers

Whilst Coade was pre-eminent in the late eighteenth and early nineteenth centuries, by 1851 it was said that 'The use of terra-cotta, or of artificial stone, as applied to objects of art and of decoration, is by no means new in this country, although such application has been of late very limited'.[140] During the nineteenth century, more than twenty-five firms are known to have been operating and by the 1870s artificial stone was being manufactured across the country from Watcombe Terracotta in Devon to William Baddeley in Staffordshire and from Gibbs & Canning in the Midlands to the Garnkirk company in Scotland.[141] Also joining the field were manufactories which were diversifying from their traditional activities, such as Doulton in terracotta and Wyatt, Parker & Co in cement. This expansion reflected the increase in demand for such products.

Blanchard

Mark Blanchard is believed to have purchased some Coade moulds in both 1839 and 1843, during that illustrious company's decline and fall.[142] Blanchard had a direct link to the Coade company, having been a terracotta worker who served his apprenticeship with Coade & Sealy before setting up his own manufactory, M. H. Blanchard & Co., in London's Blackfriars Road.[143] In an 1855 advertisement, he described himself as 'late of Coade's works and successor to them in manufacture'.[144] His company flourished from its formation in 1839 until at least 1877, for it is described as 'still carried on by him and his sons and other partners' in 1877.[145] Blanchard was awarded medals at the 1851, 1862 and Paris Exhibitions, for work that was considered 'among the best produced, either in this country or on the Continent'.[146] During the 1870s, the manufactory gradually moved to Bishops Waltham in Hampshire, allowing the company's Lambeth works to close in 1880.[147] Blanchard's planters, statuary and architectural designs drew praise from his contemporaries, including Blashfield, as being almost indistinguishable from Coade apart from the maker's stamp.[148] Although Blanchard referred to his products as being terracotta, they are actually stoneware, being a vitrified, ceramic material fired at high temperatures for long periods of time.[149] Amongst his commissions were columns for the Royal Horticultural Society gardens, whilst exports were despatched as far afield as Egypt.[150]

Blashfield

John Marriott Blashfield (1811-1882) could be described as a typical Victorian entrepreneur, speculator, artist, craftsman and technologist. Blashfield worked in the Coade tradition, producing a yellowish terracotta of exceptional hardness. He was part of the heavy terracotta industry that developed to supply the Victorians' insatiable demand for modelled building ornament and was the most successful and widely known manufacturer of the nineteenth century.

Blashfield's early life remains obscure. Born in Westminster, like Blanchard, he 'purchased some of Coade's moulds when W. Croggon closed down the original factory in 1836'.[151] These have been described as 'the best moulds'.[152] These moulds were then used at Blashfield's manufactory located in Millwall. About 1841 Blashfield entered into partnership with the Roman cement makers Wyatt, Parker & Co at a time of expansion for the firm. At the same time, Wyatt, Parker & Co issued a catalogue containing various fountains and statues in marble and artificial stone, although there is no indication which design was available in which material and whether Blashfield was involved.[153] Blashfield was personally credited with supplying the finest cement for the final phase of the Thames Tunnel. He also worked with Herbert Minton in the production of fired clay tesserae, although his involvement with the venture terminated in 1847 when Blashfield was declared bankrupt following a disastrous speculation in property development.

Despite this setback, Blashfield acquired the Millwall works of Wyatt, Parker & Co and was somehow still able to continue his cement and scagliola business. In 1851, he expanded his Millwall factory to allow for terracotta production. Blashfield claimed his decision to attend the 1851 Great Exhibition had been important as he saw the creations of Blanchard that inspired his own terracotta works. Within a short space of time he had amassed 'some hundreds of casts of good examples of ancient and modern works […] With these models, and the aid he has obtained by the employment of some of the best sculptors of the present day, he has formed a larger gallery of specimens of this order of art than has been collected since the dispersion of that of Coade'.[154] In 1853 he manufactured massive terracotta figures for the resited Crystal Palace, including *Australia* which, at nine feet tall, was the largest single piece of terracotta ever fired.[155]

Blashfield not only had a good artistic and technical grounding for his venture, he had also developed valuable contacts with prominent and rising architects, designers, and sculptors. Blashfield's 1855 catalogue contained items from both classical and contemporary sources, including some copied from Wyatt, Parker & Co.[156] The 1857 catalogue describes the origins of Blashfield's designs: 'Some of the statues and busts have been moulded from original works; others are reduced copies, from the heroic size of antiquity, carefully modelled; and several are original works by modern artists. The Vases and Tazzae are generally from modelled copies of ancient works'.[157]

Contemporaries agreed, stating that 'The vases and tazzae were most carefully modelled from ancient examples taken from the British and other Museums […] and many original designs by Mr. Blashfield and others were added […] The statues and busts, &c, are clever reproductions of ancient examples, and special works modelled for the purpose by […] renowned modern artists'.[158]

In 1858 Blashfield sold his Millwall works and had moved his business to Stamford in Lincolnshire by December of that year. The Stamford site was first developed in 1845 when the Marquis of Exeter erected an iron foundry fronted by a large monumental arch designed by a local architect, Bryan Browning. The arch, known as the Browning Arch, survives today in Wharf Road, Stamford, rather incongruously positioned as part of a new residential development which now fills the site of the former works.[159]

Blashfield and the Marquis of Exeter from nearby Burghley House became inextricably linked, for Blashfield's almost new premises in Stamford were leased from Exeter and the nearby clay resource at Wakerley was also owned by Exeter. This source of raw materials was one possible reason for Blashfield's move, the other being the lower wage levels associated with a provincial town some distance from London and bypassed by railways. Perhaps not surprisingly, the novelty of Blashfield's presence in the area attracted orders from the local gentry, including the Marquis of Exeter himself who had a large boathouse constructed at Burghley House.

Blashfield undoubtedly had a penchant for publicity opportunities, the first kiln firing at Stamford in March 1859 being attended by all the local gentry. In that first firing was a miniature bust of Queen Victoria, which was rushed to London for presentation. He also constructed a one-hundred-foot-long showroom along the north edge of the site.[160] A plan of c1872 shows four kilns.

An example of the miniature bust of Queen Victoria, which formed part of the first firing at Blashfield's Stamford works

Following his move, the 1860s proved to be Blashfield's most successful period with production increasing and new models being introduced. Amongst his illustrious commissions were urns for the Royal Mausoleum at Windsor, vases for Buckingham, Kew and Hampton Court Palaces, a colossal fountain at Crystal Palace, and copious works at Castle Ashby in Northamptonshire.[161] Blashfield's work for the Marquis of Northampton at Castle Ashby was undoubtedly his greatest commission, including balustrading with ornate piers, vast capital lettering and urns of many designs and sizes. Ironically, Doulton urns also feature in the gardens, leading to the Orangery. Blashfield even carried out much work overseas, including India, New Zealand and the United States of America.[162] Like many nineteenth-century manufacturers, Blashfield exhibited at the major international exhibitions, winning medals at the 1862 and 1867 Paris Exhibitions.[163]

By 1870, Blashfield's range had expanded to over 1,400 items and his reputation was high: 'In colour and quality the Stamford terra-cotta is of faultless excellence. The details are sharp, and in many cases exquisitely moulded'.[164] Unfortunately, this attention to detail also created problems: 'Blashfield was a perfectionist and spent an infinite amount of time on getting things exactly right, and with the state of the craft at the time wasted much time and money in replacing pieces that had shrunk in erratic ways – one of the disadvantages of his technique'.[165] In comparison to Coade stone, Blashfield's designs are considered to be not quite as durable – surviving examples of his work at Castle Ashby, for example, showing surface disintegration. After 1872, there is some evidence that there is a falling off in standards, presumably as his financial difficulties meant that he had to accept a lower level of quality so as to avoid high reject rates.

Unfortunately, a series of uneconomic contracts reduced Blashfield's working capital so that his most important foreign project, the Museum of Fine Arts in Boston, Massachusetts, proved his undoing. In 1872, Blashfield had to turn his business into a limited company, The Stamford Terracotta Company (Blashfield's) Limited, before going into voluntary liquidation in 1875. Blashfield was himself declared a bankrupt for a second time in 1877.[166] Sadly, although 'successful artistically,

Blashfield showed a remarkable lack of business acumen'.[167] After Blashfield went into liquidation, there were two attempts to sell off his works and stock, the second being necessary because of the total failure of the first. When Blashfield's moulds were finally sold, Doulton acquired a significant quantity; hence there is a direct line from Coade via Blashfield to Doulton, explaining the replication of the same designs by all three companies. Haddonstone's Jubilee Urn was adapted from a Blashfield original.

Like Coade's, Blashfield's process was incredibly labour intensive. Indeed, Blashfield's ultimate demise was not solely the result of his weakness as a businessman: 'Despite Blashfield's criticisms of the earlier schools of terracotta, he was a part of them and relied on complex clay recipes and extensive retooling after moulding and drying. Varying clay mixes meant shrinkage rates were not constant, causing much wastage'.[168]

Blashfield undoubtedly enjoyed so many successful years because, in effect, he followed the Coade business model: he used very similar production techniques; he produced high quality products; he employed the leading sculptors of the day; and he cultivated his contacts amongst the architectural profession and the gentry, no doubt assisted by his connection with the Marquis of Exeter following his move to Stamford.

Austin & Seeley

Van Spangen was a Dutchman whose terracotta manufactory in Bow was set up in competition to Coade & Sealy, flourishing from 1800 to 1828. Towards the end of the company's existence, the firm became Van Spangen, Powell and Co., manufacturing keystones, moulded panels, statues and the like.[169] Following the demise of van Spangen's business in 1828, the firm was broken up and a large quantity of models and moulds were purchased by Felix Austin (?-c1851), who set up a manufactory to make artificial stone of his own composition 'made from Portland cement, broken stone, pounded marble and coarse sand'.[170] The surface was more textured than the vitrified surface of a fired clay design, being seen as comparable to natural stone.

Austin & Seeley's display at their New Road premises, illustrating the diversity of the company's garden ornament range

This is the first recorded use of a cement-based material for the manufacture of artificial stone of this kind.

Austin's business proved successful possibly because, like Coade before him, he was shrewd enough to employ leading designers and work with influential architects. The business is recorded as having existed in New Road, Regent's Park [now Euston Road] as early as 1825, with the manufactory located near the Thames Tunnel in Rotherhithe. The New Road premises were located in close proximity to Croggon's north London branch, which has led to some historians assuming that Austin took over those premises. However, this was not the case, Croggon's premises being double the size of Austin's.[171]

Austin's mass-produced fountains and garden ornaments were praised by Loudon in the *Gardener's Magazine* in 1834.[172] Loudon also endorsed Austin's work in both his *Architectural Magazine* and *Suburban Gardener* during 1835 and 1836 respectively.[173] The company's first known catalogue dates from 1835, with the 1838 edition describing Austin's material as being 'of a light tint […which…] will not sustain injury from the severest winter'.[174] The catalogue includes a collection of designs from vases, tazzas and fountains to statuary, church fonts and porticos. Interestingly, it also makes the first recorded mention of the use of artificial stone for restoration projects, highlighting its potential where the 'ornaments of old buildings are destroyed by age, they can, by this material, be restored'.[175] Austin was obviously very confident in his material for, after just a decade of manufacture, he claimed: 'The superiority of Austin's Artificial Stone is now so firmly established, that the most eminent Architects and scientific Gentlemen have expressed, in the highest terms, their approbation of its durability, and close resemblance to the real Stone […] Specimens may be seen […] at many of the Noblemen and Gentlemen's seats throughout the kingdom'.[176]

In about 1840, John Seeley (1789-c1872) went into partnership with Austin, forming Austin & Seeley.[177] Austin & Seeley subsequently became one of the country's largest manufacturers, producing garden ornaments in a wide range of styles, even exhibiting a remarkable fountain standing over twenty feet tall at the 1851 Great Exhibition. Intriguingly, only Seeley's name appears in the official catalogue and in the company's advertisements at this time, presumably indicating that either Austin had died or had been bought out by his partner.[178] The firm was recommended for their high quality in an 1854 edition of *The Horticulturist*.[179]

Whilst, in 1863, 'Austin's artificial stone […] is generally considered to be little else than ordinary cement […] it is evidently a concrete of sand and so, cemented by lime of some sort'.[180] Austin & Seeley ornaments vary in colour from dull grey-white to a light brown-yellow. Although lacking the fine detailing of Coade or Blashfield's clay-based designs, as with many cement-based artificial stones, Austin & Seeley's designs are very difficult to distinguish from natural stone once weathered, particularly as they are infrequently marked. Products that have been identified are described as 'remarkably crisp' and 'almost unaffected by exposure to the weather'.[181] However, 'excessive cracking' has also been noted on some surviving examples.[182]

The firm was certainly still operating as late as 1872 as the *Gardeners' Chronicle* includes an advertisement for 'Austin's Stone, invented in 1826' which is described as 'Waterproof, and no sand is used in it [...] neither terra-cotta or *any other* material, whether iron or the natural stone, is so well adapted for economic decoration of gardens liable to such winters as are common to England and Scotland'.[183] The same advertisement provides evidence of the company's range, which apparently included two hundred fountains, fifty-two statues and three hundred planters.

Although numerous models were produced from antique examples, the company also had the capability to create its own designs, both Austin and Seeley being sculptors in their own right. However, other designers were also commissioned, including Papworth, Smirke and Barry.[184] Austin & Seeley was considered one of the most widely known manufacturers during the Victorian era. Commissions included the Swiss Garden near Biggleswade in Bedfordshire (now associated with the Shuttleworth Collection), Tottenham House and Longleat in Wiltshire, Marchmont in Berwickshire, Margam Orangery in Wales, Castle Ashby in Northamptonshire, Eastwell Park in Kent, Wimpole Hall in Cambridgeshire, Highnam Court and Badminton in Gloucestershire and Alton Towers in Staffordshire.

Doulton

Martha Jones, the widow of a stoneware potter, owned the Vauxhall terracotta works in 1812. John Doulton (1793-1873) worked for her for three years, having completed his apprenticeship, before he and John Watts joined her to form a partnership in 1815 in the name of Jones, Watts & Doulton. Mrs Jones retired in 1820, allowing Doulton and Watts to continue in their own name. Products were initially for household or laboratory use, although a small range of building materials had been introduced

The Doulton & Watts works in Lambeth, c1840

by the late 1820s. In 1826 the company moved to Lambeth.[185] In 1829 a special kiln was commissioned for glazed red ware and garden ornaments. Henry Doulton (1820-1897) joined the business in 1835. Inspired by the early works of Blashfield, Henry was soon attempting decorative sculpture.[186]

In 1840, a large new kiln was built, enabling the production of items including 'terra-cotta for architectural and gardening purposes'.[187] Doulton exhibited a cross section of garden ornaments at the 1851 Great Exhibition, including garden vases and statuary.[188] Watts retired in 1854, hence the change of name to Henry Doulton & Son and, ultimately, Doulton & Co.

By the late 1870s, Doulton had expanded into the manufacture of fireplace surrounds.[189] In 1878, this was said of the company: 'Doulton's works rank high, both for the beauty of their productions, the variety of designs they have introduced, and the durability and excellence of their material'.[190] Two colours were apparently available: buff and red-coloured, although the latter attracted a premium price. Regarding price, Doulton's version of the famous Warwick vase retailed at £5 5s in 1893, less than half the price of the Blashfield equivalent thirty-five years earlier.[191] Although the company seemed able to undercut the prices of rival companies producing terracotta garden ornaments, the products were nonetheless deemed to be of superb design and quality.

During the 1870s and 1880s, Doulton catalogues included vast ranges of planters, troughs, balustrading, finials, fountains, seats, lawn edgings and statuary. The latter were available in various styles, sizes (ranging from eighteen inches to over six feet in height) and prices to suit anything from country houses to suburban gardens.

Vases were one of Doulton's earliest garden products, the company's finest vase or urn being the Amazon vase.[192] Other designs included pedestals, fountains, garden seats and architectural decoration, including balustrading, keystones and capitals. In the late-nineteenth century Doulton rarely produced figurative designs, although there were exceptions, such as a set of Seasons statues.[193] In contrast, small-scale fountains formed an important part of Doulton's range. By the 1890s, Doulton was producing several vases of identical design to those previously manufactured by Blashfield, having purchased moulds when the Stamford firm went into liquidation in 1875.[194] Doulton also had a significant team of fine modellers from the 1840s to the 1930s. These included Samuel Nixon (1803-1854), George Tinworth (1843-1913) and John Broad (1837-1919).

Doulton's manufacturing process for terracotta architectural components has been described as 'quite complex'.[195] Production techniques were, in reality, similar to those of Coade and Blashfield.[196] However, the material is 'not totally impervious to the weather, and […] a less durable formula than Doulton's competitors'.[197] This did not reduce demand, as Doulton had to start producing architectural terracotta at an additional site in Rowley Regis, near Birmingham, to cope with orders.[198]

Henry Doulton was knighted in 1887, whilst the firm was awarded a Royal Warrant in 1901. However, by the early-twentieth century, Doulton's designs were adapting to reflect changing fashions. Consequently, Doulton's later catalogues are full of rather quaint designs including elves, hares, rabbits and ducks as well as coy little statuettes – a far cry from the acclaimed classical designs of the 1800s. With demand falling, production of garden ornaments ceased before the Second World War and the Lambeth factory closed completely in 1956, although the company continues to thrive in other sectors.[199]

Pulham

Rather confusingly, four generations of the Pulham family, each called James Pulham, ran Pulham's Artificial Stones. For ease of identification, these have been given the suffix I, II, III and IV in this work.

James Pulham I (c1788-1838), was born in Woodbridge, Suffolk, and spent his early life employed in the business of William Lockwood, a builder who diversified into cement production and who may have been Pulham's uncle.[200] In 1820-1821 Lockwood invented an artificial stone, which became known as 'Portland Stone Cement'.[201] This proved a great success, prompting a move to Tottenham in London where he opened 'The New Portland Stone Cement Agency'.[202] Pulham I was employed by Lockwood to run the company's works in Spitalfields, which was involved in the production of a diverse range of both garden and architectural ornaments. Lockwood retired in 1834, leaving Pulham I to take over much of his business, which then passed to Pulham's son on his death in 1838.[203] By this stage, the company was also manufacturing 'architectural ornaments such as porticos, entablatures and pediments'.[204]

James Pulham II (1820-1898) established a manufactory at Hoddesdon in Hertfordshire in the early 1840s to produce Portland cement and garden ornaments in the same medium. By the mid 1840s, the company had moved to nearby Broxbourne where a manufactory was built to allow the firm to start terracotta production to complement its cement-based range. Designs included vases, urns and other garden ornaments.

What makes the Pulham company particularly interesting is the fact that it was the only major manufacturer to produce both clay-based and cement-based artificial stone, the latter initially using Parker's Roman Cement.[205] The former were no doubt produced using similar techniques to those employed by Coade and Blashfield, being either a pale red colour or a buff, the latter being more commonly used for both garden ornamentation and architectural features. The cement-based material was deemed to have a close resemblance to Portland stone and to be excellent for both exterior mouldings and garden ornaments. Sadly, few examples have been identified, probably due to the close resemblance of the artificial stone material to its natural equivalent.

Confusingly, the term 'Pulhamite' is associated, at different times, with two distinctly different parts of the Pulham business. Firstly, there was the lime or cement render which was applied to a masonry core to create impressive rockeries, which falls outside the remit of this work. Secondly, the term is used 'in reference to a stone-coloured terracotta material, rather like Coade stone, which the Pulhams developed in the 1840s and used until the 1880s for pre-cast garden or architectural ornamentation. The term was applied [...] well into the 20th century'.[206] Pulham II himself stated that his terracotta 'was first made and exhibited at the Exhibition of 1851, with fountains, vases, &c., for which I was awarded a prize medal'.[207] Contemporaries stated 'The quality of the terra-cotta produced at Broxbourne is very high; it is hard, firm, compact, and durable, and of a soft and pleasing colour'.[208] The clay-based designs are considered more durable than the company's cement-based alternatives.[209]

The term 'Pulhamite' used c1890 on an urn at Dewstow House

The Pulham company also exhibited at the 1862, 1871 and Paris exhibitions.[210] The importance of these exhibitions is shown by the fact that the firm's c1925 catalogue is still quoting the comments of an *Art Journal* correspondent to the 1851 event: 'I do not think there is one example in the whole exhibition – British or Foreign – so perfect as yours. The material is exquisite, the design admirable, and altogether it is a most beautiful work'.[211]

In 1865, James Pulham III (1845-1920) joined the company, which then became known as Pulham & Son. By 1871, the Pulhams were employing a modest forty men and nine boys. Perhaps this was because, as a contemporary noted, 'Mr. Pulham aimed more at the quality than quantity made'.[212] Although admirable, such a policy is not generally considered sound business practice.

In the 1870s, Pulham II says his 'manufacture of Terra-cotta helps keep some of the rock-workers employed in winter, when much cannot be done outside […] and it keeps our men together through many years, as many have been in our employ 20 years – some more'.[213] As a consequence, one can assume that, by this stage, the rockery work was considered of greater importance than the terracotta. Certainly, it is for rockeries that the Pulham name is now most renowned. However, Pulham II himself still records that his 'Terra Cotta is in use at Windsor Castle, Osborne, Sandringham, Wortley Hall, Studley Royal, Dunorlan, Clifton Hall Gardens, &c, &c'.[214]

By the 1880s, the company had expanded, largely moving away from architectural commissions to concentrate instead on garden ornament and rockery work. The company's reputation was undoubtedly enhanced with the granting, in 1895, of a Royal Warrant for its work at Sandringham for the Prince of Wales. The Pulham business prospered from 1840 to the outbreak of the First World War and, although the company had moved away from cement-based production at some stage before 1925, terracotta production had continued.[215] Indeed, in the Pulham catalogue of c1925 cement-based designs are referred to in derogatory terms: 'Cement is *not* used in its composition. It is, moreover, much lighter in substance, making more elegant productions than any other so-called artificial stone. This is an important point, as the sides of a Pulhamite vase give more space for soil. It is the colour of light stone'.[216] By 1927, the company was simply advertising itself as 'Garden Designers & Craftsmen'.[217]

James Pulham IV (1873-1957) continued the family business until its closure in 1945. The manufactory was demolished in 1967 and, although a kiln and puddling wheel survive, family and company records have not. This presents numerous problems for later historians. For example, the date of birth for James Pulham I is given variously as 1765, 1788 and 1793 – a variation of twenty-eight years. Whilst his death is generally agreed to have been in 1838, this means he could have been aged anywhere between forty-two and seventy-three years when he died.

The Pulham catalogue of c1925 shows 'a continuing line of vases and fountains but, gradually, the repertoire came to include seats, balustrades, sundials, bird baths, pergolas and the layout of whole gardens in the fashionable styles of the time'.[218] One of the company's most impressive designs was exhibited at the 1862 exhibition - an imposing tiered fountain derived from a marble original now in the Villa Petraia near Florence. Intriguingly, this design featured a combination of both clay and cement-based components. Another fine original design created by Pulham in its clay mix has now been rescaled and replicated by Haddonstone in a cement-based material, being known as the Westonbirt vase by Pulham and the Westonbirt urn by Haddonstone. Pulham's standard range typically included fountains, vases, pedestals and architectural details, with many of the sculptures being reproductions of antique, Renaissance, as well as contemporary subjects.

As late as 1917, one author bemoaned the fact that, whilst 'much interest has been manifested of late in ornamental concrete, and so little seems to be known about the unlimited possibilities of the artistic treatment of this material' the artificial stone industry was in terminal decline, disappearing almost completely by the time of the Second World War.[219] Today, the only company of note that continues with a limited range of garden ornaments in the Coade tradition of terracotta is Ibstock

Haddonstone's version of Pulham's Westonbirt vase

Hathernware. Formed in 1874 as The Hathern Station Brick Company, it is now better known for ornamented building exteriors to complement the brickwork of the parent company, although a 'range of urns, vases, statuary' is claimed on a dormant page of the company's website.[220] The decline in the use of terracotta-based artificial stone is largely as a result of the rise of the cement-based alternative, which is less labour intensive to produce and, consequently, more affordable.

Chapter IV

Manufacturers since World War II

A growing appreciation of the past and the resultant need to conserve historic landscapes and gardens, as well as a desire from the public to create their own accurate representations of gardens from the past, led to the re-emergence of artificial stone manufacture during the latter years of the twentieth century. However, a recent commentator noted that 'only a few manufacturers in the UK are able to produce reasonably faithful replicas of nineteenth century models. Others produce items that are embarrassing and unnecessarily poor in design and materials [...] Twentieth century cast-stone containers, when well designed and manufactured should be as durable as their nineteenth century counterparts'.[221] Unfortunately, a visit to any garden centre will soon introduce the most casual observer to a proliferation of hopelessly designed and clumsily produced garden ornaments in artificial stone as well as concrete, plastic and terracotta. Sadly, these poor representations are accepted by the majority of the public who remain ignorant of the few manufacturers of quality. These include Chilstone and Haddonstone, whose history was briefly intertwined.

Through the latter part of the twentieth century, 'ambitious stone or simulated stone structures have had recurrent periods of popularity in larger gardens whenever the taste for formality has re-emerged. This is reflected in the supply of simulated stone products, including columns and entablatures'.[222] The resurgence in the use of the material is because 'artificial stone [...] assumes the form of decorative features of the real thing. They were manufactured throughout Europe; particularly in Italy, France, where numerous designs were advertised in mail order catalogues, and England, where two popular varieties called Chilstone and Haddonstone were produced'.[223] This is the first time a history of either of these two companies has been attempted.

Chilstone

The post-war revival of artificial stone can be attributed to Michael Dibben (1929-1985) who founded the Chilstone company in 1953.[224] Gaynor Gilbert, his partner, relates how Dibben opened an antiques shop in Salisbury that regularly sold old garden ornaments when he saw someone restoring an old Jensen sports car with fibreglass, and wondered whether he could use that same technology himself. Apparently, Dibben's father and grandfather had been involved with the manufacture of cast iron garden ornaments, which required the use of sand moulds, and so he investigated whether he could do the same with a simple sand and cement mix packed into fibreglass moulds. Dibben himself is reputed to have made his first mould at the age of just ten. Educated at the Portsmouth and Central Schools of Art, he studied architecture and developed his skills in casting and mould-making. Although fibreglass technology was certainly not new, it would appear that Dibben was the

Reproduced by kind permission of Hugh Palmer

Chilstone's Pope's urn, a replica of a design attributed to William Kent for Alexander Pope's garden in Twickenham

first to successfully utilise this technology for garden ornament production, the earliest items produced being ball- or sphere-shaped finials for gate piers. This was followed by the Tulip urn, which remains in the Chilstone range today.[225]

Around 1956, Dibben moved from Salisbury to London where he briefly worked as an interior designer in Halsey Street off the Kings Road before moving to the country for both space and health reasons soon afterwards.[226] Chilstone's first proper home was, therefore, Great Linford Manor in Buckinghamshire, which Dibben leased and lived in whilst also using the property as offices. Until this time, artificial stone production was very low key and the company took some years to grow. Twin stables at the Manor served as production facilities, whilst the grounds to the north and east formed a show garden. The property is now completely surrounded by the expanding Milton Keynes, whose development corporation compulsorily purchased the site even though the premises still survive as an integral unit. Chilstone exhibited at the Chelsea Flower Show for the first time in 1968 and was a regular exhibitor until the early 1990s. In 1971, the company still employed only eight people and everything, even the mixing of the raw materials, was done by hand. By that time, the range comprised some fifty designs, including the company's famous replica of a design attributed to William Kent at Alexander Pope's Twickenham garden.[227]

Whilst still at Great Linford, in an attempt to boost sales, Chilstone took on Robert 'Bob' Barrow (1932-1996), whose family leather-tanning business, Barrow, Hepburn & Gale, was in decline, like so many shoe-related industries in the country. Barrow was taken on in 1971 as Chilstone's de-facto Sales Director and was encouraged to stay by way of various financial and shareholding inducements, which never materialised. At one stage, Barrow was even accepting garden ornaments in lieu of salary. This was, at least in part, because the company always had funding issues.[228] Chilstone moved to the National Trust Sprivers estate in Kent during 1976, the same year that Gaynor Gilbert first became involved with the business. Barrow's diaries record that the 'Great Linford Sale' occurred on 23 June 1976 and that he visited the premises on 5 January 1978, presumably after Chilstone had vacated.[229]

When Dibben died from leukaemia in 1985, ownership of the company was split into three, with Dibben's sons, Damian and Justin, becoming Directors and Gaynor Gilbert Managing Director, although the sons apparently took no active part in the business. This unsatisfactory arrangement continued until Gilbert bought out the sons' shares and, in 1996, the company moved to Victoria Park near Langton Green, Tunbridge Wells, Kent.[230] Here is located the company's factory, yard, offices and show gardens, which were officially opened by Alan Titchmarsh in 1997. The site comprises some thirty-five acres, which were owned by Gilbert personally.

Although the company trades as Chilstone, its accounts have previously been filed under the name of Hesway Limited since incorporation on 22 May 1968. The name Chilstone is believed to derive from Chilworth Manor in Hampshire, which had a family connection.[231] Hesway had two Directors, Gilbert (1953-), appointed in 1991, and her husband, Graham Gilbert (1962-), who was appointed in 2003.[232]

Whilst the Victoria Park site would be difficult to develop further owing to various restrictive covenants, in September 2007 the company and its assets were sold to Steptrack Ltd., whose business is described as 'Development & Selling of Real Estate'.[233] The new company directors are Philip Haynes and Graziella Guaglio-Haynes.[234] What the future holds for the Chilstone company is currently unclear.

Amongst Chilstone's most prestigious projects were the supply of 138 urns to Kew Gardens, eight gate pier capitals for Buckingham Palace, balustrading for Clarence House and Hever Castle, as well as garden ornaments for Woburn, Vine House and Longleat. Today, the standard range includes replicas of designs ranging from planters, sundials, bird baths, statues, fountains, furniture and obelisks to architectural features including balustrading, gate piers, landscape structures and porticos.

Chilstone adheres to the basic production techniques of its founder, being a mix of 'natural aggregate BS882', otherwise known as building sand, and 'ordinary Portland cement BS12' to which 'Water reducing agents' are added.[235] This allows the production of a single off-white standard colour. Although pigments can be used to create darker colours on request, it must be assumed that the creation of lighter colours, such as a Portland stone equivalent, are difficult or impossible to recreate. Chilstone views itself predominantly as a garden ornament manufacturer, the company's claimed cube compressive strength of 22-25 MPa being, at best, just able to comply with the 25MPa requirements of British Standards, although well under the 35MPa level required by the United Kingdom Cast Stone Association. In 1970, the Financial Times described Chilstone's products as the 'best reproduction, "antique" garden ornaments' although the same article describes the finished products as 'softish, and rather rough', an attribute which is still typical today.[236] Chilstone's 1972/1973 catalogue describes the company's products as follows: 'Each Chilstone ornament is handmade in reconstituted stone by a special process, developed to ensure a finished texture indistinguishable from natural stone. The colour and texture of the material is midway between Portland and Bath stones, and its soft composition encourages the spontaneous growth of mosses and lichens […] This important characteristic ensures that each ornament blends in harmoniously with its setting'.[237]

Chilstone has an unusual policy with regard to mould creation and maintenance. Firstly, it does not have the capability to create its own moulds and is therefore reliant on outside contractors. Secondly, the company does not maintain a master set of models, instead relying on display pieces in the show garden. As a consequence, when a mould deteriorates and needs to be repoured, rather than going back to a pristine model, the company turns to a piece in its show gardens, which has already weathered. For this reason, standard Chilstone designs often fail to have sharp details. Whilst some regard this as desirable when the design has taken on the patina of an antique, this finish can look unacceptable when new or when needed for architectural applications.

Chilstone has survived for fifty-five years, having established a niche for itself in the marketplace. Chilstone has also spawned a number of minor local rivals, including Abacus Stone, Classical Stone, T.H. Little and Voustone, some of which use the same mould-making company as Chilstone. Perhaps most significantly, the company's history is also intertwined with Haddonstone, the most important manufacturer of the late-twentieth and early twenty-first centuries.

Haddonstone

Bob Barrow, the founder of Haddonstone, was educated at Wellington College, Berkshire before briefly studying medicine at Queen Mary College in London and then joining the family business, travelling to India to learn about leather and its manufacturing processes. Returning to England in the mid-1950s, Barrow was appointed to run Barrow, Hepburn & Gale's Northampton and Leicester offices. However, he resigned in 1968 when he discovered his route to becoming the company's Managing Director had been blocked by a nepotistic appointment. With a young family to support, Barrow strove to find an avenue where he could utilise his business, marketing, promotional and personnel skills, selling everything from make-up and ice cream to roofing and greenhouses over the next couple of years. He also had investment and property interests. It was at this time that Barrow first met Peter Keig, who was to have a profound impact as a friend, adviser and consultant.[238] He is first mentioned in Barrow's diaries as early as January 1972.[239]

Feeling his skills were not providing sufficient reward, a frustrated Barrow took the step of advertising himself as an experienced businessman looking for a senior position and equity stake in a business. The advertisement brought Barrow six responses, each of which was followed up with a visit. His favourite was a specialist boat builder in Oundle called Fairline, which is now renowned for luxury boats. When that arrangement floundered, Barrow turned to another company on the list, a small garden ornament producer run by Michael Dibben called Chilstone. Barrow spent six months building sales and reorganising the company, whilst also boosting marketing and public relations activities. Despite investing money in Chilstone, it soon became apparent to Barrow that the promised equity stake was not going to materialise.[240]

As late as October 1971, Barrow was being described in *The Observer* as the business partner of Dibben at Chilstone. The image that accompanied the article tells us much about the characters of the two men, who are shown sitting on Chilstone Vine urns outside Great Linford Manor. Dibben sits nonchalantly, hair slightly dishevelled,

Bob Barrow and Michael Dibben outside Great Linford Manor

casually dressed with a fashionable neckerchief, every inch the artist. Barrow, meanwhile, is dressed in a shirt and tie, neatly groomed and with the slightly bemused expression of someone who is unused to such frivolous poses, yet remaining every inch the astute businessman.[241] The relationship between two strong personalities, each pulling in a different direction, was always destined to end acrimoniously and Barrow was the one who made the move, correctly believing that he could create a successful business without Dibben. Dibben's actions in purchasing a new car with the proceeds of the increasing sales, rather than reinvesting funds to expand the business, proved to be the last straw for Barrow.[22]

Initially the registered name of Barrow's new company was Iudex Limited, although it has always traded under the Haddonstone brand. Over the years the registered company names have switched for various accounting reasons, Iudex changing its name to Haddonstone Limited on 19 December 1978, a new company called Adenwood Limited being created to act as the holding company on 24 July

1986, with Haddonstone Limited becoming the trading company at the same time. The prefix for the Haddonstone brand was taken from the village of East Haddon where Barrow lived in The Manor, surrounded by extensive grounds which he soon developed to become the company's acclaimed show gardens. The

Aerial view of Haddonstone's acclaimed show gardens at East Haddon in Northamptonshire

catalogue entry for the 1972 Chelsea Flower Show, where the new company was allocated a prestigious Main Avenue site for its first exhibition, is for Iudex, the corresponding description stating: '"Haddonstone" Garden Ornaments, Paving Stones and Screening Stones'.[243]

The following account of Haddonstone's development draws heavily on the company's Board Meeting notes, Annual Report and Accounts, diaries and interviews with key staff. None of these avenues would be available to anyone outside the company's Main Board as they contain much commercially sensitive information. As a consequence, unless otherwise noted, all such confidential sources will simply appear in the endnotes as coming from the 'Haddonstone Archives'.[244]

Although the first report and accounts for Iudex state that 'The company was incorporated on 4th April, 1972', the company must have been establishing its collection of designs and marketing materials in late 1971 if it was able to launch at Chelsea in May 1972.[245] Indeed, notes from 1986, in Barrow's own hand, state that he employed Malcolm Pollard, described as a 'sculptor lecturer' in October 1971, the same month that Barrow appeared in *The Observer* alongside Dibben as a partner in Chilstone! The same handwritten notes state that Pollard 'got together ex-students to work at Manor in prod[uction] […] Oct 71 – May 72 under MP [Malcolm Pollard], models and moulds were made by him and team of graduates. Barbara Wykes started then as well [and is still employed as a freelance sculptress by the company]. John [Liczman] worked in evenings in Jan 72 building up stocks of products ready for Chelsea launch. Sold £2000 worth. Original Range: Plaited, Eliz, French, Regency, Scaled, Vention Vase, Seat'.[246] In less than six months, Barrow had designed a range of garden ornaments, made models and moulds, designed a stone mix, manufactured products, created a brochure and designed an exhibition stand, whilst also setting up an office and production facility and taking on employees. This was undoubtedly a major achievement. However, these efforts were nearly in vain as Chilstone issued a writ in an attempt to stop Barrow exhibiting at Chelsea, principally claiming that he had copied their stone formula. The legal challenge failed as Haddonstone had developed its own unique formula, having consulted with various industry experts. Most obviously, the Haddonstone mix included a significant proportion of limestone, whilst Chilstone's did not.[247]

The date of Pollard's commencement is given as 27 March 1972 in Barrow's diaries, although this may simply indicate that he was working on a freelance basis until that time.[248] Pollard became a non-shareholding director on 1 January 1973 in order to supplement the fledgling company's design capabilities, although he is never recorded as attending board meetings.[249]

The earliest surviving Haddonstone catalogue dates from autumn 1972, comprising a folder with seventeen loose-leaf sheets, mainly in black and white. It opens with the words: '"Haddonstone" seeks to enhance the home and garden of the more discerning person, by recapturing in re-constructed stone some of the architectural splendour of the 16th, 17th, 18th and early 19th centuries'.[250] Interestingly, the price list is given in both sterling and US dollars, showing the company's interest in exports from its earliest days. The first seven designs, which had remained unidentified until this current research, are illustrated, although the range had already expanded to include fifty unique pieces. Below are listed the full names of the first seven designs with their 1972 prices.[251] For interest, if the design is still manufactured, the 2009 price for the same design is shown in parentheses.[252]

Plaited basket	£9.50	[£70]
Elizabethan jardinière	£25.00	[£255]
French urn	£19.50	[£255]
Regency urn	£9.50	[£107]
Scaled jardinière	£27.50	[£263]
Vention vase	£75.00	[no longer manufactured]
Straight 51" seat	£20.00	[£288]

For comparison, the prices for the two original designs that had equivalents in the Chilstone range show their version of the French urn [the Vine urn] as being £28 and their equivalent of the Regency urn [the George IV tazza] as £13. Although the Chilstone prices have been taken from a Spring 1974 catalogue, this still shows that Haddonstone was either aggressive in its pricing strategy, able to manufacture more economically, or both. The first Report and Accounts show sales of £47,644 for the first sixteen months, with an impressive fifteen per cent being ploughed back into marketing the business via advertising, brochures and exhibitions.[253] The importance of good design and sound marketing strategies are therefore evident from the earliest period in the company's existence, policies that have been followed to this day. Some of Haddonstone's first advertisements appeared in *Country Life*, a magazine that still forms a key part of the company's advertising schedule.

Barrow's early diaries show how quickly he established a network of contacts, many of whom still work with the company today - companies such as Clifton Nurseries, Waddesdon Manor, Belvoir Castle, Notcutts garden centres and the Chewton Glen Hotel, all appearing alongside names such as Arabella Lennox-Boyd, the journalist Fred Whitsey and Roddy Llewellyn.[254] 1975 saw the company's first prestigious commission, the supply of replica finials to Margam Park in South Wales as part of European Architectural Heritage Year. The Margam Swagged and Margam Masked urns remain in the Haddonstone Collection today. In September 1976, Alison Lowe is first recorded as travelling with Barrow to East Anglia to visit stockists, a role which Lowe continues to fulfil today as Director of Ornamental Sales. As well as Chelsea, a variety of other exhibitions are recorded, including the Stockport Flower Show, Harrogate Show and GLEE, where the company still exhibits to the garden centre market.

Barrow's 1986 notes detail the early development of the company at this time: 'Manufactured in garage for 2½ years, working from Manor, moved to Dovecote old laundry premises 2½ years'.[255] The original Dovecote Laundry in Harlestone closed in 1974, the licence between Viscount Althorp and Iudex, whereby the Laundry could be used as Haddonstone's manufactory, being signed in November 1974.[256] Barrow's notes continue: '1976 converted garage → flat and office, moved office out of home. Moulds in old woodwork shop. RHB [Bob Barrow] doing deliveries, took on pt time driver and hired vehicle from May 73. First purchased van in 1974 pt time driver. Full time driver not until 75. Moved to present factory in 1979. Moved to old forgehouse – offices and mould shop in 1979 – little later within 6 months'.[257] The premises in Upper Harlestone were leased from Earl Spencer for a period of thirty-five years from March 1979. At that time it is stated that forty people were involved in the business.

Barrow's 1986 notes also reveal the pioneering impetus of the company, which was 'Creating fresh markets thro' demonstrations of the flexibility of our product in

67

The Upper Harlestone factory, originally used for Haddonstone production and later utilised by both Arcadian Garden Features and Haddoncraft Forge

where c[ast] stone not previously recognised in architectural and restoration field and interiors. Standard range of classical stonework constantly increasing, range of classical statues in pipeline, more export exhibitions being considered, constant research into new mouldmaking techniques'.[258]

One of the key moments in Haddonstone's development was undoubtedly the opening of its manufactory at Brixworth in Northamptonshire. Purchased in September 1986, the premises were officially opened by HRH Princess Alice on 3 December 1987, after HRH Princess Margaret had to cancel. The attendance list for the ceremony included many local dignitaries, business associates and employees, including sixteen employees still with the company today. At that time, the company employed over fifty people and exported to more than twenty countries.[259] These included Dubai and Bahrain, where Barrow travelled as early as 1976 to exhibit the company's wares. In 1983, a distribution agreement was signed with Seahorse Trading for the US market, an agreement that later proved difficult to terminate and thereby allow Haddonstone to set up its own company in the States. In Australia, Chilstone's former distributors decided to go into partnership with Haddonstone instead although, by 1990, Haddonstone was attempting to dispose of its interests. The Australian company now simply pays a licence fee to use the trade-marked Haddonstone name.

A surviving letter dating from 1986 outlines the company's insightful understanding of its marketplace: 'The direction in which we are heading is the professional designer market, catering for the institutional and rich private client, which suits our operation well. We are more flexible than most manufacturers, our designs are adaptable and we are able to cope with the more demanding (but not so fastidious) architectural market […] direct sales of garden ornaments are up and we are still and shall always continue to improve our range (and quality) of garden ornaments […] Many of the top designers now consider us trend-setters'.[260] As the company exploited the opportunity to develop into the architectural market, whilst also continuing to target high-earning private clients, the late 1980s saw the most rapid expansion experienced in the company's existence, trebling its sales in just three years.[261]

Board Notes of November 1987 detail the appointment of new directors, namely James Barrow (Barrow's nephew), Adrian Coles and David Lakin. Immediately, a new management structure was being proposed for the manufactory, a new vehicle was ordered, a new sales order processing system was initiated and the bungalow adjacent to the company's East Haddon offices was noted as being near completion for use by the accounts department. Coles was appointed acting Managing Director during Barrow's absence in early 1987, an opportunity taken by James Barrow to break away to form a rival business which ultimately floundered and disappeared. September 1988 saw the appointment of David Barrow, the founder's son, and Alan Lorentzen as Directors.

Board Notes of April 1989 show that Barrow recognised the problems which can result from an expanding company as well as the need to continue moving forward: 'RHB asked all Board members to give due consideration to what course the company should follow in the future […] RHB reminded the Board of the need to maintain adequate communication between departments as the company continues to grow'. After discussions, in June 1989, it is reported that 'the company objective should be to optimise our profitability from the existing dry-mix reconstructed stone business'. In a short time, the latter policy would change considerably as the company sought to diversify.

Haddonstone first started to seriously review its options in the important US marketplace in October 1989 when it was 'proposed that a new company, Haddonstone Inc., should operate from Berryville [Virginia] (possibly with other premises on the West Coast)'. It was hoped that Haddonstone could work with Seahorse, the company's US distributor, to expand their business and it was proposed that 'an existing Haddonstone employee be transferred from the UK for an extended period to oversee the operation'.[262] This personnel policy ultimately proved successful. The same Board Meeting also saw Bob Barrow become Chairman, allowing Coles to become Managing Director. As Barrow's health declined, June 1990 saw Coles first chair a Board Meeting whilst Barrow was present. As early as January 1990, it was identified that 'the East Haddon offices were approaching capacity' and the stables at nearby Holdenby House were seriously considered as alternative accommodation, although these plans never came to fruition. Instead, both the main office and adjacent bungalow were expanded.

Following the breakdown of protracted negotiations with Seahorse undertaken by Coles and Keig, Haddonstone decided to form its own company in the US, headed by James Scott-Bowden, who was recruited specifically for the purpose. In September 1990, the first container is recorded as being en route to the new US office and warehouse in Bellmawr, New Jersey. At the same time, Haddonstone was looking towards the reunified Germany as a potentially lucrative export market. Ultimately, an office would be set up in Baruth, near Berlin but in the old East Germany, which meant even essentials such as telephone lines proved a problem, necessitating the opening of a sales office in nearby Zossen in June 1992. Unfortunately, Baruther Fassadensteine GmbH, which was set up with a German partner, never achieved its objectives and, even though Haddonstone had taken control by June 1993 and set up a new company called Haddonstone (Deutschland) GmbH, severe personnel problems led to the company's closure in 1994.

A joint venture between Haddonstone and the conservatory company Marston & Langinger saw the launch of Orangeries at the 1989 Chelsea Flower Show. Derek Sampson was appointed Production Director in November 1990 and Haddonstone briefly entered into the custom joinery and bronze patination business under the name of Haddoncraft, a brand that would ultimately be reused for the company's wrought iron company. These ventures would ultimately all prove unsuccessful but show how aggressively the company was exploring every avenue to achieve sales during a time of worldwide recession. Despite these efforts, in October 1991, the company laid off a small number of factory staff for the first time in its history and even the annual dinner dance was cancelled, partly to save costs and partly to show employees just how critical it was to keep costs under control. Further redundancies were made in April 1993. Throughout this period, Haddonstone continued to spend significant sums on marketing, including printed literature, exhibitions and advertising, knowing that this policy would ultimately ensure that the company would come out of the recession with a better market share than before and realising that competitors were suffering even more severe problems. By May 1993 it is reported that the factory had recommenced a forty-hour week and 'overall morale is excellent' although, in December 1993, reference is made to the 'continuing poor performance of the group, with Haddonstone well behind target and USA and Germany making losses'.

David Lakin left the company in 1991 to be replaced by Eric Lennox, who was appointed Financial Director the following year. Meanwhile, the US company struggled to find effective leadership to take the company forward, parting company with Scott-Bowden in 1992 and then trying to find a successor from both inside and outside the business, including Sampson, Michael Judge, Richard Dennis and Lorentzen during a period of less than six years. Also in 1991, Haddonstone became a founder member of the United Kingdom Cast Stone Association.

Haddonstone considered expanding into wet-cast production in September 1992 although, at the time, the 'Board felt that any involvement in the wetmix market (even using a totally separate company) was downgrading Haddonstone's image as an upmarket company'. With hindsight, this shows two interesting facets of the company: firstly, the company's keen awareness of the importance of brand image; and, secondly, that the company is prepared to change its mind if circumstances change. Wet-mix production is now an important part of the company's business, production commencing in 1995, the same year that Peter Hartley became Production Director. Under the trademark of Haddon-TecStone, now normally shortened to TecStone, this process is used to manufacture a range of designs including statues, fountains, fireplaces and steps.

In November 1992, Haddonstone was offered the opportunity to acquire both Chilstone and Minsterstone, the latter a well established cast stone business in the South West, probably best known for fireplaces. Chilstone again approached Haddonstone with a view to selling in December 1997. Coles and David Barrow visited and 'felt it was a good location, with a good showgarden and retail sales area. However, the production facilities and procedures were poor'. A month later, after more detailed site surveys had been conducted, reference is made to the site being 'very restrictive and future development is extremely unlikely. The value placed on the site is very much less than that required by Mrs. Gilbert' and negotiations were abandoned.

Haddonstone USA expanded in 1993 with the opening of a further office and warehouse in California to service the potentially lucrative West Coast. With the US market expanding, Haddonstone then looked to produce in the States rather than continuing to ship all products from England. Consequently, following extensive research to find the best location, it was decided to manufacture in Pueblo,

Colorado. The agreement was signed on 24 April 1996. Described as 'the largest single investment the company has ever made', within a year the factory was fully operational with twenty-seven employees.[263] The first stone was produced from the new Pueblo factory in June 1996.[264] After past management problems, it was decided that the US company should consolidate by operating less autonomously, with significant input from the UK, headed by Coles. This continued until it was felt possible to set up a formal US management structure with Andrew Maslin, a former UK manager, being appointed President in 2004. The US company now makes a significant contribution to the Haddonstone Group, handling the important Pacific Rim market that had formerly been dealt with from England. The Californian warehouse closed in 2005, being considered surplus to requirements once the Colorado operation was fully staffed.

By this time, Bob Barrow had passed away in November 1996 after a long illness, being succeeded as Chairman by Peter Keig, who had been Vice Chairman since February 1992. In the Board Meeting notes of November 1996 it is recorded that 'David Barrow spoke about Bob's sad and untimely passing. It is intended that the structure of the Company and its business is to be continued as in the past. The company had been Bob's life for the past twenty years, and it is hoped that it will continue to prosper even though Bob is no longer at the helm'. In April 1997, Neil Sparrow was appointed Contracts Director, having been with the company since 1985.

Simon Scott was appointed Marketing Director in 1999, having joined the company as Marketing Assistant in 1989. Since 1989, the company's catalogue has grown from 88 to 208 pages, showing how the standard range has diversified and expanded. One other important part of Scott's role was the design and creation of displays at the world-famous Chelsea Flower Show, where Haddonstone had first shown in 1972 and most following years. For fifteen consecutive years, from 1989 to 2004, the company exhibited at this prestigious event, culminating in the creation of two medal-winning Show Gardens, both designed by Scott. Each of these exhibits had a theme, as listed below:

1989 ....Orangery
1990 ....Venetian Folly
1991 ....Italian Courtyard
1992 ....Chambers' Ruin
1993 ....Garden of the Elements
1994 ....Raphael Pool
1995 ....Temple of Pan
1996 ....Naiad Fountain
1997 ....Isola Bella
1998 ....The Belvedere
1999 ....Millennium Garden
2000 ....Garden of the Seasons
2001 ....Orangery
2002 ....Elysian Garden
2003 ....Oasis of Ruin [Show Garden]
2004 ....The Knot Garden [Show Garden]

The company ultimately pulled out of the Chelsea Flower Show as it moved from being a commercially important exhibition to a celebrity-based event. Other shows where Haddonstone has regularly exhibited include GLEE, Decorex, Interbuild [until 1999], Batimat [until 2003], Homebuilding & Renovating [since 2005] and BBC Gardeners' World Live [since 2005].

In 1999, Haddonstone once again actively looked to expand into new markets. In 2000, as a direct consequence, the company set up two new businesses: Arcadian Garden Features and Haddoncraft Forge. The designs in the Arcadian range were, almost without exception, the work of Simon Helm, who had been utilised to supplement the activities of Wykes since 1994. Arcadian no longer trades as a separate company as the range proved successful enough to be incorporated within Haddonstone's main collection from 2006. The other company to be formed was Haddoncraft, which made wrought iron gates, railings, garden furniture and landscape structures alongside the Arcadian production facility at the refurbished

In 2003, Haddonstone created its first show garden at the world-famous Chelsea Flower Show

factory in Upper Harlestone. In 2009, both operations transferred to the main Brixworth site. A less successful venture was Haddonstone's involvement and subsequent acquisition of the Glass Houses conservatory company, which saw the recommencement of the Orangeries business, being launched at the 2001 Chelsea Flower Show. Glass Houses became part of the Haddonstone Group in July 2003, before being placed in voluntary administration during September 2006.

Since the late 1990s, Haddonstone's core business has been thriving again; the US company being awarded its largest ever contract in 2003 for the supply of $750,000 of architectural and ornamental stonework for a magnificent private residence in Singapore. The UK secured a similarly sized order in 2005 for the supply of custom architectural stonework for a major retail development in Ireland and, in 2009, achieved a £1,000,000 order for the supply of landscape ornaments and balustrading to 'The Pearl' in Qatar.

Haddonstone's acclaimed showgardens continue to attract visitors from around the world. In July 1996, planning permission was granted for a major expansion of the gardens to include a new site on the other side of Church Lane from the main East Haddon offices. Now known as the Jubilee Garden, being named in commemoration of the company's Silver Jubilee, the garden opened in 1998 and contains a gothic grotto, pavilion and temple. At Brixworth, the company installed a state-of-the-art vapour-curing system that was operational from February 1999, whilst land adjacent to the manufactory was purchased in 2000 in preparation for future expansion. Those plans were temporarily suspended to allow investment in Pennine Stone, a new company formed in 2002 to produce cast stone architectural dressings for the volume house building market. The impressive production facility is located near Doncaster in South Yorkshire.

Peter Keig passed away in January 2003, his role as Chairman being taken by David Barrow. In August 2008, Tony Mason was promoted to Production Director. This was the most recent change in Directorship at Haddonstone, there having been fifteen executive and non-executive Directors in the company's history:

Robert Barrow	1972-1996		
Jane Barrow	1972-1988	Peter Keig	1989-2003
Malcolm Pollard	1973-1979	Derek Sampson	1990-1993
James Barrow	1987-1988	Eric Lennox	1992-present
Adrian Coles	1987-present	Peter Hartley	1995-2006
David Lakin	1987-1991	Neil Sparrow	1997-present
David Barrow	1988-present	Simon Scott	1999-present
Alan Lorentzen	1988-1997	Tony Mason	2008-present

It is not just senior management that has remained remarkably stable. In 2004, analysis showed that an amazing forty-seven per cent of Haddonstone employees had been with the company for more than ten years.[265] In 2008, three employees were awarded with special long service awards for more than twenty-five years service – Nita Attwood, Alison Lowe and Tony Mason.[266]

Interestingly, it is not just employees who stay with the company for long periods. Of the company's first seven designs, the Elizabethan jardinière, French urn and Regency urn all remained in the top twelve best sellers in both the UK and USA as recently as 2006, showing the longevity of good design. At that time, Haddonstone's top-selling design in the UK was the Clarence urn, whilst in the US the Westonbirt urn proved supreme.[267] It is also interesting to note how many of Haddonstone's designs have been replicated from their illustrious predecessors. The list below details the name of Haddonstone products that, through present researches, are now known to have been previously created in some form by other companies, followed by a list of those previous early manufacturers.

Ascott urn: ....Pulham
Eagles: ....Doulton
Griffin plaque: .... Coade
Ham House pineapple: .... Coade
Jubilee urn: ....Blashfield, Doulton
Large acanthus urn: .... Doulton
Lotus vase: ....Blashfield, Doulton
Margam swagged urn: ....Coade, Austin & Seeley
Naiad: ....Coade, Croggon
Seasons plaques: .... Coade
Sphinx: .... Coade
State vase: .... Blashfield
Tatham tazza: ..Coade & Sealy, Wyatt & Parker, Blashfield, Doulton
Versailles vase: .... Blashfield
Victorian jardinière: ....Austin & Seeley
Westonbirt urn: ....Pulham
Wilton urn: ....Austin & Seeley

From this analysis of past and present sales literature, it can be seen that the Tatham tazza has been in production for around two hundred years and has been manufactured by at least five different companies, using both clay and cement-based artificial stone. Numerically, at least six Haddonstone designs have been reproduced from Coade originals, and five each from Blashfield and Doulton. This may explain why 'Haddonstone is often regarded as the modern successor to Coade Stone'.[268] This exercise also reinforces the lineage between Blashfield and Doulton, the latter acquiring the former's moulds, as three of the designs from this relatively small sample passed from one company to the other. The heritage of the artificial stone industry remains important to this day. In 2005, Haddonstone

The Tatham tazza, manufactured by at least five different companies from the eighteenth to the twenty-first centuries

even introduced a Clifton Coade Collection with faithful replicas of both Coade and Doulton designs. This shows, once again, how good designs can continue across the centuries. Interestingly, research has shown that it is also possible to identify various sites where successive owners have used artificial stone over time: Highnam Court in Gloucestershire, for example, incorporates the work of Austin & Seeley, Pulham and Haddonstone.

It is intriguing to record how many designs successive artificial stone manufacturers replicated through the centuries. The Coade sphinx, for example, was produced in marble in seventeenth-century France, in lead in eighteenth-century England, by

Haddonstone is the latest in a long line of manufacturers to replicate the Faun with Pipes statue

Coade where it appears in their catalogue of c1784 and by Austin where it appears in its 1835 catalogue.[269] The Coade version has now been copied by Chilstone, albeit with a changed head, and by Haddonstone. Sir Gavin Hamilton excavated the Warwick vase near Rome around 1770, before it was restored and sold to the Earl of Warwick. Subsequently, both Coade and Blashfield duplicated the design.[270] Both Coade and Blashfield also created versions of the famous Borghese vase.[271] The Faun with Pipes has been much replicated in both lead and artificial stone, most recently by Haddonstone.

Recent commentators have noted that 'Throughout the country, Haddonstone has been used on a number of National Trust properties, including Waddesdon Manor and Ham House, along with Haddo House and the House of Dun for the National Trust for Scotland. In many cases, Haddonstone replicated a garden ornament, for example an urn, statue, fountain, balustrade or finial, from an original eroded piece'.[272] Many designs originally commissioned for historic properties have become part of Haddonstone's extensive collection. Notable locations include the Ascott Estate, Cliveden, Eastwell Manor, Leazes Park, Margam Park, Shugborough Hall, Warwick Castle and Wilton House. As a consequence, Haddonstone has developed 'an immense range of products from classical temples and colonnades through to fountains, seats and ornaments from the great styles and traditions of European gardening'.[273]

In 2006 Haddonstone started manufacturing cast stone reinforced with glass fibres under the TecLite brand. This allows manufacture of designs with thinner walls, which are consequently lighter. Although designed primarily for architectural applications, this method is also used to manufacture a number of Haddonstone's contemporary garden ornaments.

With one eye on the past and one eye on the future, Haddonstone is now generally regarded as a 'world-renowned manufacturer of cast stone [...being...] a popular choice among professional garden designers'.[274] When comparing Haddonstone with others, it has been said that 'there are those that are faithful reproductions of eighteenth and nineteenth century pieces and then there are those that are embarrassingly poor. Haddonstone is one company that by and large has accurately copied originals, often by taking moulds of them. They produce a range that even includes temples and porticos. The detailing on the classical orders even looks right!'[275] This is why Haddonstone achieved pre-eminence towards the end of the twentieth century, a position it has held in the early years of the new millennium.

Chapter V

Perceptions Through Three Centuries

Changing perceptions of artificial stone have existed through the centuries. Manufacturers, in particular, have always harked back to a mythical time when artificial stone was respected and admired. As early as 1730, Richard Holt commences his treatise with a grovelling six-page dedication to the Earl of Burlington, who he hopes will help him *'raise again Artificial Stone* to its *old Lustre* and *former Credit'*.[276] Holt also refers to the 'common Defects in the best *Natural Stone,* and extraordinary Faults in all the *inferior Kinds'*.[277] In particular, he criticises both Portland and, in particular, Bath stone, likening both of these famous natural stones to cheese![278] Holt's own patent claimed that his material was 'more durable and harder than stone and Marble, insomuch that neither Wet or Dry, neither Frost or Snow, Heat or Cold in the Extremity, can do damage to it', claiming his artificial stone as being 'of very great Use and of Publick Benefit in all our Dominions […] by reason of its Cheapness as well as its Goodness'.[279] These are undoubtedly the two most common claims for artificial stone over time: superiority over the natural equivalent and the potential monetary savings to be made.

In 1770, Daniel Pincot was scornful of the works of his contemporaries, describing the 'vast heap of execrable ornaments (if I may call them ornaments) found about most of our English Buildings'.[280] However, he maintains the artificial stone producer's mantra of cost and inferior natural equivalents, stating that 'it is a certain and well-known fact, that the weather in this island has so destructive an effect on Portland, Bath, and other rock stone'.[281] In addition, 'artificial stone […] has a just claim to the attention of every builder, not only on account of superior strength and beauty, but of cheapness also […] The saving here is very considerable over natural stone, and that in proportion to the enrichment'.[282] However, Pincot is the first to identify serious resistance to artificial stone, principally from within the ranks of the stonemasons who presumably felt their livelihoods were under threat if artificial stone succeeded:

many fresh instances of disingenuity, prejudicial to this manufacture, have occurred [...] Many of the masons, and some other workmen, particularly the lesser masters, (for some of the greater deserve praise) notwithstanding they are conscious of superior merit in this manufacture, yet are using their utmost efforts to overturn it; and that by practices so mean that I am almost ashamed to mention them.

One measure they take is by deterring modellers from working for the manufactory; telling them that they will be despised by the whole trade, as forwarding a work it is their interest to suppress.

Again, when their employers signify an inclination to use this material, they immediately cry out, O Sir! why will you have artificial stone? nature must certainly be better than art; it is but an imitation, and a meer makeshift. Is it not more to your credit to have real stone than to stick up lumps of earthen ware?[283]

In reality, the comparatively low cost of artificial stone has often encouraged building works incorporating both natural and artificial stone to proceed when the cost of natural stone alone would have made a project prohibitively expensive. An example of this occurred in 1990 at Malvern College Chapel in Worcestershire, where a stonemason realised that there were pinnacles at two levels that needed replacing. Rather than carve each from scratch he contacted Haddonstone to obtain a price for custom stonework and won the contract, which also involved considerable amounts of one-off carved stone items where artificial stone would probably have been uncompetitive.

A fascinating extract from *The Times* of 1785 typifies the variety of opinions held by contemporaries regarding the material, these words being from a correspondent who had visited Coade's factory to find that the designs were taken

> *from the most valuable masters of antiquity, and executed in a stile he had no conception of in this country. He found that it meets with the most flattering encouragement from the Nobility [...although...] Architects and Builders, who are chiefly connected with stone masons, rather discouraged the use of it. Its durability in the most intense frost is, however, he finds, such an argument in its favour, that he thinks it only wants to be more generally known; to be universally introduced [...] several other Manufactories passing under the name of Artificial Stone Manufactories, have been established [...] but which dropped off one after another, and their productions have been ascribed to this; especially in one instance, the gateway leading to Sion House, in the road to Brentford, from which, in the opinion of our correspondent, as well as several others, this Manufactory has received irreparable injury.[284]*

The Syon Park gateway became a *cause célèbre* for the artificial stone industry and seems to have coloured opinions on artificial stone through to the present. The Duke of Northumberland had commissioned one of Coade's rivals [possibly George Davy, who had taken over Pincot's original works in 1767], to create this gate, yet had to call on Coade to make extensive repairs. Coade generated much publicity by loudly claiming that their product was superior to that of their competitors, which made it all the more embarrassing when the firm was twice called back to repair their own badly deteriorating stonework, the results of which are still visible today.[285] This high profile project caused severe embarrassment to the industry, including the Coade company, which had no responsibility for the original problem.

This was a great shame as, over the centuries, Coade ornaments have generally resisted the effects of weathering far better than natural stone. In 1859, even Blashfield felt moved to comment that 'wherever it has been used it is now found more perfect than stonework adjoining, of the same date'.[286] Today, Coade ornaments are rightly regarded as fine works of art, where the character of the material was appreciated, properly expressed and soundly designed. Indeed, compared to natural Portland

The Syon Park gateway became a cause célèbre for the artificial stone industry

and Bath stone, Coade has a greater sharpness of detail and a greater resistance to weathering. However, there are a small number of examples that have split along their joint lines, presumably because of poor manufacture.[287] Despite these reservations, Coade stone is deemed 'remarkably successful and examples of it are to be found in the work of all the best architects of the time'.[288] Indeed, 'Such was the texture and colour of Coade stone that, once in place, it was indistinguishable from stone itself'.[289] Perhaps the final word on Eleanor Coade should be reserved for Alison Kelly, her acclaimed biographer, who states that 'Eleanor Coade's elegant product reflected the taste of the period in which many people consider that the heights of British applied arts were achieved, and added its own lustre to them'.[290]

Many contemporaries actually wondered why replicas of fine designs from antiquity were not more widely seen. William Shenstone, for example, puzzled why replica 'statues are not more in vogue in our modern gardens. Though they may not express the finer lines of an human body, yet they seem perfectly well calculated, on account of their duration, to embellish landskips, were they some degrees inferior to what we generally behold. A statue in a room challenges examination, and is to be examined critically as a statue. A statue in a garden is to be considered as one part of a scene or landskip'.[291] Although post-Classical works were considered wanting in terms of truth, politeness and other aspects of quality, it is not surprising to discover that artificial stone ornaments became so popular in gardens of this period. Indeed, this demand was driven, at least in part, by the increasing number of wealthy industrialists and others all over the country with money to spend on beautifying their gardens and, as artificial stone was considerably cheaper than marble or real stone, it proved a popular choice.

In 1836, 'Loudon stated that the use of vases and other garden ornaments in artificial stone was now "very fashionable" [...and...] Fowler mentioned that during the 1840s artificial stone was in "very extensive use"'.[292] Despite this popularity, as early as 1855, Blashfield bemoaned the fact that, although 'manufacturers have begun to mould and imitate ancient Greek works of this high class [...] little advancement is made. The public taste is scarcely yet at so high a standard, and the few good copies manufactured have frequently remained unsold'.[293]

Blashfield also suffered from a public who seemed satisfied to accept a lower quality of work than his own, for there was a 'reaction against the ultra-fine finish of [...] terracottas in favour of something less refined and more vigorous. During the 1860s the balance between the old and new schools tipped in favour of the latter. The rougher-textured terracotta, straight from the mould, using only single fire clays and grog to control shrinkage rates, found much favour and produced a considerable economy. With fashion and economics against it, the old school was doomed'.[294]

Yet, in 1877, Pulham was criticised for having introduced, in 1843, 'what is termed granulated terra-cotta, having the appearance of stone. Latterly this imitation has fallen into disrepute, and wisely so, for although where terra-cotta is now used it is adopted instead of stone, yet it is not used to *imitate* stone, but passes for what it is, - *bona fide* terra-cotta'.[295] This distinction is important as it does show that terracotta, for all its undoubted qualities, was not regarded as a material to imitate stone but to provide an alternative to stone.

Undoubtedly, the demand for artificial stone ornaments in terracotta-based materials began to dwindle by the end of the nineteenth century, manufacturing being on a much smaller scale than it had been in the previous century. The laborious manufacturing process undoubtedly hastened this decline. Of renowned manufacturers such as Doulton, for example, it was said that:

> *This necessarily slow process and the possibility of kiln disasters meant that delivery dates to the building sites were often erratic. This was the main objection raised against the material as its use became widespread; otherwise it fitted most of the requirements of the Victorian architect. It was more economical than stone [...] It was as strong as stone, although this was often disputed by its opponents despite frequent tests which proved its high crushing strength. It was more durable than stone, being better able to withstand the atmospheric corrosion in the new cities. Despite the materials obvious practical advantages, some architects discredited it on aesthetic grounds, maintaining that 'crockery cubes' were not a sufficiently dignified building material. The architectural press did much to disperse these doubts, printing lengthy articles about the impressive historical pedigree of terracotta.*

> *John Ruskin, the eminent art critic, was in favour of the material and helped raise its status by stressing the craftsmanship involved [...] It was really the practical example set by distinguished architects Barry and Waterhouse which convinced others of terracotta's suitability for important public buildings.*[296]

In 1868, even Blashfield recognised the threat to his production techniques from cement-based products, feeling it necessary to justify his higher prices: 'vases of a very large size are made at a cost little exceeding the production of similar objects in cement and other plastic materials'.[297] Indeed, as the twentieth century dawned and cement-based manufacture became more widespread, the *Stone Trades Journal* in 1904 commended cast stone as a substitute for stone in all areas.[298] However, fashion moved on and, during the early years of the twentieth century, there was a drift away from the formal garden ornaments so popular with the Victorians. As a consequence, the artificial stone garden ornament industry had spiralled into decline by the time of the Second World War.

In reality, throughout the greater part of the twentieth century, both artificial stone and real stone were swept aside by the enthusiasm for exposed concrete. The ACA deem it 'ironic that at the same time as reconstructed stone was being used with classical detailing in imitation of real stone, the pioneers of the Modern Movement were exploring the potential of concrete as a structural material'.[299] Indeed, concrete 'was *the* material of the twentieth century'.[300] However, in 1926 it was stated that 'Architects associated the words "patent stone" with the cheap and nasty, and it was not until a few of the leading architects began to experiment with the new material that it was in any way considered by the rank and file'.[301]

The *Architects' Journal*, in 1932, when comparing Bath stone to its artificial equivalent, identified that 'the reconstructed material is […] much more durable, and has no natural bed, so there can be no flaking of the surface. It is unaffected by sea air, and the face is not destroyed by a sulphurous atmosphere'.[302]

In 1942, the architect Charles Holden wrote in relation to cladding rather than ornament in artificial stone. His comments are still noteworthy: 'Reconstructed stone may be appropriately used when there is much exposed structural concrete in a building, as for example in copings but to use such reconstructed stone for ashlar work as a means of getting a stone faced building on the cheap is a dismal sham and I would like to see architects refusing to be party to its use in this way. If we cannot use genuine stone let us use good honest brick which we can afford and not spend our energies in perpetuating and in encouraging others to perpetuate a false use of what is otherwise a good serviceable material which has some potentiality for beauty when properly handled'.[303]

In the immediate aftermath of the Second World War, classical architecture was held in contempt, probably as a reaction, whether consciously or subconsciously, to its associations with fascism. With the populace weary of wars, the mood amongst architects and government was for the creation of a new utopia, fast. As a consequence, much of the architecture of this period was modernist and bereft of high ornament. This principle lasted into the 1960s, Giles Worsley commenting that the 'guiding principle of the Sixties was contempt for the past'.[304] It was against this background that Chilstone struggled in its early years during the late 1950s, whilst Haddonstone thrived in the 1970s, helped by the public's violent reaction against the modernist movement. Whilst this oversimplifies the complex architectural movements of the period, there can be no doubt that the time was right for an artificial stone revival in the 1970s and 1980s.

By the late 1980s, perceptions were changing once again: 'cast stone has come a long way since then [the early 1960s] and some feel that the best look so like the real thing that they could threaten the future of the stone industry'.[305] However, the ultimate success of any building material depends not just on the manufacturer but also on the design by the architect and on the skills of tradesmen on site, for 'Cast stone may, when properly designed, manufactured and installed, be as durable as many natural stones'.[306] Whether the movement away from exposed concrete structures to ones of brick and stone has stimulated the cast stone industry or whether it is the availability of better quality cast stone which has encouraged architects, developers and clients to make use of the material, is almost impossible to ascertain. Whilst the replacement of an old artificial stone garden ornament with a modern equivalent in cast stone is the least controversial application for the material, the material undoubtedly has much more to offer for both restoration and recreation projects. For this reason, by 1989, *The Journal of Preservation Technology* was describing the material as being 'fully accepted'.[307]

Many modernists thought of ornament as no more than a passing fashion, quickly out of date, even though it has survived, with modifications, from ancient times. Alfred Loos was one of the most radical architectural theorists of the early-twentieth century, as can be detected from the mere title of his influential *Ornament and Crime,* published in 1908. In it he states that 'We have outgrown ornament […] Ornament does not heighten my joy in life or the joy in life of any cultivated person […] not only is ornament produced by criminals but also a crime is committed through the fact that ornament inflicts serious injury on people's health, on the national budget and hence on cultural evolution […] ornament is wasted labour, power and hence wasted wealth. It has always been so'.[308] This radical manifesto for a modern world, free from the constraints of past architecture and ornament, proved very influential, leading Filippo Tommaso Marinetti to state, in 1914, how 'I oppose and despise […] All classical, solemn, hieratic, theatrical, decorative, monumental, frivolous, pleasing architecture'.[309] And the Congrès Internationaux d'Architecture Moderne to declare in 1928 that 'Works of architecture can spring only from the present time'.[310] As a consequence of this radical shift in architectural theory, artificial stone manufacturers struggled to survive in the early-twentieth century as their *raison d'être*, namely classical ornament, had become deeply unfashionable, even though Le Corbusier expounded the merits of the production technique: 'serial manufacture enable these elements to be made precise, cheap and good'.[311] Reflecting modernist thinking of the early-twentieth century, lavish and unnecessary use of ornament was waspishly described by Horace Walpole in 1782 as 'impotent displays of false taste'.[312]

Ultimately, the counterblast to the modernist view did not occur until the 1970s, or even the 1980s. Intriguingly, this perfectly correlates with the formation and expansion of the foremost practitioner of artificial stone today, namely Haddonstone. The greatest exponents of traditional architecture in this period included Leon Krier, Demetri Porphyrios and Prince Charles.[313] Leon Krier believed 'The terms classical architecture as against modernist so-called "architecture" are contradictory, antagonistic and incompatible propositions: the first based on artisan-artistic production, the latter based on industrial modes of production'.[314] Ironically, in many ways, the manufacture of artificial stone in a classical style actually bridges this barrier. Provocatively, Allan Greenberg espouses the theory that 'Classical architecture is the cutting edge of architecture for the 21st century because it is the most comprehensive and the most challenging approach to architectural design and city planning. Because it is rooted in the physiology and psychology of the individual human being, the Classical language of architecture is always modern'.[315] On a more basic level, Roger Scruton simply states that 'The building of a human face in architecture depends not only on details, but also on materials. These should be pleasant to the touch, welcoming to the eye and accommodating to our movements'.[316]

Prince Charles entered the debate in the late 1980s, stating that classicism 'is not the simple pastiche that some critics claim it to be: learning the classical language of architecture does not mean that you only produce endless neo-Georgian-style houses. Classicism provides an incredibly rich inventory of infinite variety'.[317] Where the system fails the artificial stone producer is that the manufacturer is a mere servant to the wishes of the architect or client. Whilst companies such as Chilstone and Haddonstone have extensive ranges of designs, mainly replicating the proportions of antiquity, there is also a custom-made capability that accounts for around thirty per cent of Haddonstone's current UK production. What the manufacturer cannot control, however, is the ultimate use of their products by their client. However technically advanced the product, however exquisite the detailing, if the client wants to create a pastiche monstrosity then the manufacturer, as a commercial organisation, will inevitably acquiesce. The manufacturer cannot act as the arbiter of taste.

Artificial stone continues to polarise opinions. Typical of the vehement rejection of artificial stone by local authorities is a case in a Cotswolds village as recently as 2007, a planning inspector rejecting an appeal on the grounds that 'the use of artificial stone had compromised the character and appearance of the conservation area [...] its use would not preserve and would certainly not enhance the character or appearance of the area'.[318]

Notwithstanding such criticism, artificial stone 'ornaments are consistently mistaken for natural stone and vice versa'.[319] The late David Hicks observed that 'There is a great deal of false snobbery attached to garden ornaments, the feeling that if they are not fine original works of some antiquity, then they are not worth having. It is not a snobbery I can share [...] If your tastes lie more in the direction of urns and vases, then there are a number of manufacturers who make excellent reconstituted stone ones at reasonable prices'.[320] Whilst Hicks considers it 'snobbery' to reject artificial stone out of hand, others take a contrary view.

In *Noblesse Oblige*, edited by Nancy Mitford, the phrase 'U and Non-U' was used to distinguish upper-class language from the rest. The phrase passed into the language to define upper class and non-upper-class behaviour. In 1996, James Bartholomew introduced a gardening equivalent in his book *Yew & Non-Yew*. This humorous volume asks: 'What are your garden sculptures made of? a) Bronze or stone b) reconstituted stone (as per Haddonstone, Chilstone or similar) c) plastic, polystyrene or concrete d) you have no sculptures'. The scores are: a) 4, b) 1, c) minus 3 and d) 1.[321] The book later questions:

> *Is Haddonstone Yew? Haddonstone, Chilstone, and Minster are companies which make objects that look like stone. But these objects – seats, pots, urns, statues and so on – are really made of reconstituted stone [...] But is "fine cast stone" Yew? It is certainly tempting for the Yew gardener. These companies know which buttons to press. They do everything they can to make gardeners think, believe or at least hope that their products are Yew. They [...] explain that a statue is a precise replica of an eighteenth-century one at such-and-such a noble house. An advertisement by Haddonstone boasts of "traditional English quality" and "classic designs" [...] The trouble is, the eighteenth-century urn you buy from Haddonstone is not the real thing. They know it. You know it. We can't get away from it. It is Non-Yew.*[322]

In 2003, two leading experts at Sotheby's wrote: 'The popularity of antique statues, seats, urns, and fountains has never waned, and the market for these has risen steadily over the last 15 years'.[323] This is later qualified with the comment that 'Composition stone urns are very affordable and should weather quickly so that they look old, however, they will not increase in value in the same way that an antique urn will'.[324] This comment is at odds with prices achieved at Sotheby's auctions that have seen Haddonstone designs achieve significant increments in value. In 1992, the Daily Telegraph identified that 'garden statuary to be included in an auction of expensive architectural antiques are modern reproductions […] still manufactured in large quantities to identical designs. Apart from a light growth of moss and algae on some of the less exposed surfaces, the only difference between them and the factory-fresh urns, planters and statues in Sotheby's sale […] is the price'.[325] Various guide prices are then compared with Haddonstone retail prices to show a premium of more than one hundred per cent. It is believed that these inflated prices are largely due to the limited number of legitimate antiques available for sale, making weathered replicas of premium value. For even Sotheby's experts have gone on record to state that, once 'established in a garden it is difficult to spot that it is not a carved-stone original'.[326] However, some designs that are auctioned are undoubtedly not antiques, one of Haddonstone's Eton College Fountains being sold at Sotheby's within one year of it being launched by the company in 1993. As a consequence 'If one was uncertain whether the statue was cut from stone […] it could easily be mistaken for one made from a cement-based artificial stone'.[327] As cement-based artificial manufacturers have gone to great lengths to ensure that their products closely resemble natural stone there have, as a consequence, been 'countless incorrect identifications'.[328]

Publicists for the artificial stone cause, such as Blashfield, noted that: 'Of late years stonework appears from some cause to decay more rapidly than heretofore. This may be from the increased consumption of coal, and coal gas […] The stone buildings which have been erected in London during the last thirty years, are in a lamentable state of premature decay; and in some instances the only exposed details in a perfect state found in such structures, are those which are made, not of stone, but of Coade's terra cotta'.[329] Written by Blashfield just fifteen years after the demise of his illustrious predecessor, this is a remarkable testimony to the works of Coade

92

and an indictment of the capability of natural stone. In effect, Blashfield was calling for a modern material for the modern world.

Sadly, the major heritage bodies exacerbate this problem today as the policy of both English Heritage and the National Trust is to replace like with like, whatever the long-term implications. In other words, if natural stone was used originally and has now eroded badly, it will still be replaced by natural stone as close as possible to that original material even though that will, in turn, need replacing. Artificial stone alternatives are rarely considered and, consequently, the problem is perpetuated.

Published technical advice from English Heritage states: 'The choice of replacement stone must be both sympathetic and cost-effective. Wherever possible compatible materials should be used – stone that closely replicates the original in its appearance, chemical, physical and mineralogical properties, strength and durability'.[330] From this statement, the preference is, quite rightly and logically, for natural stone to be replaced when required by identical natural stone. However, this statement certainly does not preclude the use of artificial stone provided it can display the same characteristics as the natural equivalent although, in practice, artificial stone use in such circumstances is rare.

Likewise, an English Heritage consultation document identifies that 'The historical value of places depends upon direct experience of elements that have survived from the past, but it is not easily diminished by change or partial replacement as evidential value'.[331] The same document states: 'Evidential value, historical values and some aesthetic values, especially artistic ones, are dependent upon a place retaining (to varying degrees) the actual fabric that has been handed down from the past; but authenticity […] can relate to design as well as fabric […] The design may be recoverable through repair or restoration, but perhaps at the expense of evidential value'.[332] These seemingly contradictory statements do seem to allow the use of materials other than those originally used, provided they are technically and aesthetically suitable. Indeed, although artificial stone is not mentioned, an intriguing example of a far more modern material is given in the same document:

'The substitution of timber sash windows for PVCu ones in the façade of an 18th century house, in order to return it to its known appearance a decade ago, rather than the conjectural appearance in the 18th century, is likely to be justifiable'.[333] It would seem easy to contend that such an action would be far more detrimental than using artificial stone in an equivalent scenario. Indeed, 'The use of materials or techniques with proven longevity and which are close matches for those being repaired or replaced, tends to carry a low risk of future harm'.[334] This statement would seem to support the use of artificial stone. Evidential value is defined as 'Relating to the potential of a place to yield primary evidence about past human activity' elsewhere in the same document.[335]

In the 1990s much research relating to artificial stone was undertaken by the University of Dundee, the potential importance of this being recognised by Building Design in 1990: 'The Dundee programme may well lead to concrete as architectural cast stone being reinstated as a high quality 21st century building material'.[336] The Dundee programme culminated in a joint research programme by the University of Dundee and the United Kingdom Cast Stone Association, making a number of interesting conclusions relating to artificial stone when compared to natural stone, in effect stating that both materials are generally comparable: 'All Cast Stone products, and particularly when waterproofed, were found to be highly resistant to carbonation. Efflorescence did not occur in any of the test samples and weathering in Cast Stone was similar to that in control natural stone. The data also suggests that dry-cast, Cast Stone is no less vulnerable to frost attack than natural stone'.[337]

Two senior National Trust regional curators were consulted by telephone to ascertain their current opinion, as the Trust has no formal advice relating to artificial stone.[338] Both had similar thoughts, namely that the general policy of the Trust was to replace like with like wherever possible. In other words, if the original statue were carved stone from a particular quarry then the preference would be to use stone from the same quarry to create the replacement or provide elements to enable an acceptable repair. Somewhat bizarrely, if this were not possible then fibreglass would be seriously considered as at Chiswick and Stowe. Quite why such an alien material would be considered ahead of an artificial stone is unclear. However, there are exceptions, the example of Downhill in Northern Ireland being offered. Here, two heraldic figures were originally carved with the strata running vertically so as to give strength to rather slender legs. Over time, this has compromised the rest of the figure to such an extent that an artificial stone replacement has been commissioned via a conservation workshop in order to avoid replicating the past problems with natural stone. Both National Trust curators stated that they had no prejudice against the use of artificial stone, most decisions being taken on a local rather than a regional or national level. If cost were a critical issue then the possibility of using artificial stone would increase if multiple castings were required. Currently, however, the preference is to proceed with restoration projects only when full funding is available, thereby reducing the opportunity to use artificial stone, unless, of course, it is an artificial stone design that requires replacement. This may explain why companies such as Haddonstone have not recently had significant commissions from the Trust, whereas in the past the company has undertaken the following replication work:

Reproduced by kind permission of Haddonstone Archives

Haddonstone replicated statuary, urns and finials for Lyme Hall in Cheshire

finials for Antony House; two different urns for Ascott; urns at Cliveden; finials for Dogmersfield; pineapple finials at Ham House, replicating Coade originals; custom urns at Ickworth House; statuary, urns and finials at Lyme Hall; vases for Shugborough; and parapet screening to the main tower at Waddesdon. The majority of these designs are now in Haddonstone's standard collection, the arrangement for this being made at the time of the original commission.

English Heritage officers concur with their counterparts at the National Trust, stating, from a landscape perspective, that 'There is no specific policy on the use of artificial stone as such and decisions will be site specific and based on the significance of the stone or artificial stone feature. Highly graded registered gardens, listed buildings or scheduled monuments will demand greater care [...] Cost is always an issue'.[339] Regarding artificial stone in relation to buildings

> *The underlying technical premise of our [English Heritage] conservation policy is the use of new materials that are physically and chemically compatible with the current condition of old ones (such as water vapour permeability in external masonry materials for example). This is to prevent inadvertent damage to historic fabric. This will, of course, be related to specific characteristics, such as current condition, vulnerability and exposure [...] Appearance and weathering characteristics of a new material introduced into an old building are other issues, and would in many instances lead to the specification of natural materials rather than fabricated ones [...] It may be difficult to source appropriate stone for historic building repair, due to closure of quarries or the depletion of geological strata. This might prompt consideration of the use of artificial stone.[340]*

The Association of Conservation Officers 'do not generally recommend the use of artificial materials in the repair of historic buildings. The two main problems they foresee are appearance and lifespan [...Indeed...] using cast stone in the repair of a Listed Building is regarded as a change of material and would therefore require Listed Building Consent'.[341] This is why many owners, unable to afford carved stone, have to remove deteriorating original stonework on the grounds of health and safety without replacing it, thereby destroying the historic integrity of the design whilst keeping within Listed Building regulations. An example is a Grade II listed house in North Yorkshire where parapet balustrading on three towers were deemed to be unsafe, a previous owner having removed some sections which were in imminent danger of collapse. The new owner wanted to replace the balustrading but was met with significant opposition.

The Inspector of Historic Buildings, English Heritage Yorkshire Region, stated that 'We consider that the use of artificial stone such as Haddonstone would seriously undermine the architectural integrity of the historic fabric, and […] the match is likely to be poor in the longer term'.[342] Commenting on the same restoration project, the Yorkshire Dales National Park Authority, whilst acknowledging 'that Haddonstone has been used on some impressive buildings' believed that 'our policies may well be substantially more stringent than those of other Authorities. I have no problem with the quality of the material, I am sure it is a very fine product, but it is not natural stone, it does not weather the same way as natural stone, its appearance may be similar now but will it be after 20 years of weathering?'[343] Unfortunately, it would appear that the ignorance of the true composition and weathering characteristics of fine quality artificial stone will remain for the foreseeable future, with the actions of those tasked with the function of preserving our heritage being directly responsible for the deterioration of country houses and their gardens where owners cannot afford to embark on restoration due to the high cost of natural stone. This is particularly frustrating with restoration projects where, even if stone from the original quarry can be extracted, it will not be from the same strata and so it simply cannot match the original.

There are examples, such as the Haldon Belvedere in Devon, where English Heritage has insisted on the use of certain traditional methods only to find they were not durable. Elsewhere it would appear that conservation bodies would, rather perversely, prefer to see a building crumble rather than allow a logical solution which involves compromise yet saves the structure, such has occurred at the Clavell Tower in Dorset.

Whilst stone is aesthetically suited to the English garden as it blends so well with the landscape, artificial stone has often been considered as 'mean'.[344] During the nineteenth century new materials, including artificial stone and cast iron, largely usurped Portland stone.[345] However, there has always been a fear of the new with the largely conservative building market. Even the use of natural Bath stone, now highly regarded, was vehemently opposed in the eighteenth century, with architects such as Colen Campbell and Nicholas Hawksmoor publicly stating that it was 'unable to bear any Weight, of a Coarse Texture, bad Colour, and almost as Dear as Portland Stone'.[346] Indeed, in 1862, the Royal Institute of British Architects, when discussing artificial stone, stated: 'Sandstone is no more than a concrete of sand […] limestone, on the other hand, is concreted on a different principle'.[347]

As a consequence, in 1857, Blashfield wrote: 'Much enquiry and discussion have recently taken place on the durability of stone and other substances, for external architectural work in this country. It is said that a great deal of the granite disintegrates and crumbles; that marble and stone decay in a few years, and that metal easily corrodes; but it is said that well-burnt Terra Cotta withstands the ravages of time unimpaired; the only secret to ensure its durability being that of sufficient firing'.[348] Some modern commentators actually group artificial and carved materials together, feeling that they weather in such a similar manner. For example: 'Ornaments in cast, carved and composition stone attract lichens and moss more readily than a smooth material'.[349] Unfortunately, the debate, whilst fascinating, would not appear to be able to reach an obvious conclusion, the dichotomy of views seemingly polarising opinion.

Conclusion

On the basis of the foregoing analysis in the main body of this study, it is now possible to reassess the status and perception of artificial stone through the centuries. It is also possible to reassess the importance of key figures such as Richard Holt. As it is a moulded product, whether cement or terracotta based, artificial stone offers the opportunity to create intricate designs and patterns which would either not be possible in carved stone, or would be prohibitively expensive. Undoubtedly, one of the chief advantages artificial stone has over its natural equivalent is cost, particular when multiple castings are required. The expansion in the use of artificial stone was undoubtedly the direct consequence of the demand for a competitively priced alternative to natural stone. As techniques developed, the standard and quality of some designs became so high that they are almost impossible to distinguish from their natural equivalent, resulting in incorrect attribution. Artificial stone, like natural stone, can be subject to deterioration, but this should not inhibit its use as it is just replicating its natural equivalent, albeit in a predictable and controlled manner. All building materials change in appearance with time, an acceptable change in appearance being one where the material mellows with age. Cement-based artificial stone has the ability to mellow with age although both artificial and natural stone will appear new when first installed.

As early as 1770, Daniel Pincot identified the refusal of some to accept that an artificial stone can be superior to its natural equivalent: 'there are some persons so obstinately averse to the introduction of whatever they imagine has but the air of novelty, that they will be both blind and deaf to the plainest demonstration'.[350] He found this incredibly frustrating as he believed that 'artificial stone […] though the outward appearance is nearly the same, the internal properties are totally different, and far superior to all the common sorts of rock stone'.[351]

Today, there continues to be a complete dichotomy of views when it comes to artificial stone. John Fidler, formerly of English Heritage, wrote in 1992:

> *On the question of cast or reconstructed stone, the battle lines are firmly drawn. The real purists cast aspersions on the artificiality of reconstituted material, calling it fancy concrete by another name, an aesthetic disappointment, a threat to natural stone production and a fad supported only by the visually impaired. But the fact is that today there are reputable companies producing very passable likenesses of authenticated designs with great technical integrity and marketing aplomb.*[352]

Whilst for great periods in the early twentieth-century, the reputation of artificial stone was rightly tarnished by poor detailing and weathering problems, the industry still suffers from that image even though new manufacturers have emerged who produce high quality products with none of the problems of their forebears. It was these problems of perception that drove key manufacturers together to form the United Kingdom Cast Stone Association in 1991, which sets higher standards than those required by British and other international standards. Unfortunately for contemporary advocates of artificial stone, whilst poor artificial stone is rightly vilified, good artificial stone so quickly takes on the appearance of natural stone that it is often mistaken for, and assumed to be, natural stone and so is not given the acclaim it deserves.

Each generation seems to have regarded artificial stone as a new invention, rather than as a material with a long and illustrious past. For this reason, each generation has to re-establish the credentials of the material. Indeed, 'fabricated stone in the hands of capable designers could be used with a frankness which was in no sense imitative, but which relied on the quality of the material itself for its artistic expression'.[353] In the late seventeenth and early eighteenth centuries, antiquarianism led to a tremendous revival of interest in facsimiles of classical designs and motifs. The Georgians yearned for the look of stone even when they could not afford the real thing. Consequently, budding entrepreneurs experimented with numerous types of terracotta formulae, later using cements and binders in order to develop a method of cold-casting artificial stone. From 1800 onwards there are innumerable references to different artificial stone inventors and manufacturers, each carefully guarding their composition. Just as we today hear of some magic ingredient in a shampoo or toothpaste, the same was true for the pioneering artificial stone manufacturers, who used all kinds of pseudo-scientific gobbledegook in their promotional literature in order to differentiate themselves from their competitors. This is why Coade can now be said to possess 'legendary qualities', even though its success lay more in the choice of designs, materials, preparation and skilful firing than any magical ingredient.[354] Indeed, the likes of Eleanor Coade made a product that so closely resembled natural stone that natural stone is what most spectators, including many 'experts', believe they are viewing, making attribution very difficult.

However, it is Richard Holt's influence on the formation of the artificial stone industry that, I believe, needs to be reassessed, as I consider that he should be recognised as the founder of the industry, not Eleanor Coade. He is certainly a far more important figure than previously credited. As long ago as 1770, Daniel Pincot stated that there did not 'appear to have been any revival of this business till about forty years ago, when a considerable undertaking […] was set up by one Mr. Holt, at Lambeth'.[355] Recently, Richard Smith has even challenged the attribution of many Coade designs, stating that 'Holt and Pincot's work could be confused with Mrs Coade and Alison Kelly, the doyen of the latter factory, can be understandably confused.'[356] In evidence, Smith notes that in a comprehensive list of 371 examples of Coade stone 'just 10% of the listing were signed and dated.'[357] Smith believes that Richard Holt was probably the illegitimate son of Thomas Holt (1682-1745), the steward/agent for the Dukes of Bedford.[358] As a consequence, Richard Holt would have been well positioned to conduct business with a high level of clientele well before Coade's arrival on the scene. At locations such as Chiswick House, this could even provide the key to the attribution of the urns, terms and herms which are known to have been in position since the 1730s, thereby predating Coade.[359] Does Holt's gushing dedication to Burlington suggest that it was he who manufactured these ornaments?

Eleanor Coade's importance in the history of Georgian decorative art and architecture should not, however, be underestimated, as she was the first key protagonist. Sir John Soane, for example, used Coade stone from the age of twenty-seven until he was seventy-five.[360] The Coade company's history coincided with the neo-classical period and virtually ended with it as well. The firm's elegant designs reflected the taste of a period in which many believe the British achieved their zenith in terms of applied arts. The classical revival of the late-twentieth century suffered from the stigma of its association with fascism, as well as a reaction against its style largely because it was popular – popular in the sense that it can be understood and accepted. However, the classicists have a standard bearer in the form of HRH Prince Charles who believes that 'when a man loses contact with the past he loses his soul […] If we abandon the traditional *principles* upon which architecture was based for 2,500 years or more, then our civilisation suffers'.[361] Classicism is a style of repeated elements that are often rather complicated to make, making mass production expensive, except in the case of artificial stone. In many ways, the rise of Chilstone and Haddonstone in the late-twentieth century reflected the rising of classical architecture like a Phoenix from the ashes of modernism. By the end of the century, a balance between these two diametrically opposed architectural styles existed and a 'new ornamentalism' movement now exists whereby classical motifs are being reinterpreted for contemporary use.[362] Whether such a compromise situation is ultimately successful will be interesting to review over the coming years.

Whatever one's personal thoughts on whether artificial stone is a successful substitute for natural stone, it is an undeniable fact that, just as good and bad artificial stone has been produced over the centuries, good and bad natural stone also exists, varying in quality with the fissures and density variations inherent in any natural material. Indeed, modern experts state: 'No natural stone is capable of resisting the elements, and although many may appear to be in relatively good condition, the effects of even one hundred years' exposure on something as robust as Portland will have worn a substantial part of the original detail away. Less durable stones will have suffered far worse'.[363] However, a significant problem for artificial stone remains: 'Like many new substances, it had begun life as a substitute for something else and could not shake its connotations of "second best"'.[364] Indeed, in many ways artificial stone is not fully accepted by either modernists or traditionalists. It often replicates ornament, particularly classical or traditional ornament, and for this reason is unacceptable for modernists, yet because it is man-made rather than natural it also fails to be fully appreciated by traditionalists.

Gerhard Auer's insightful comment that 'Building materials are artificial by nature' reveals the paradox inherent in any criticism of artificial stone.[365] Brick and glass are accepted yet are just as artificial. Carved stone is accepted, yet a building never uses this natural material in its natural form, being cut, sawn or carved by man to create unnatural shapes. Yet artificial stone has always been treated with suspicion. Pincot noted this irrational thinking as early as 1770 when he rhetorically queried: 'I might ask whether our forefathers called the introduction of glass in windows a makeshift, as this was artificial, and horn was natural'.[366] The reason for this long-held aversion to the use of artificial stone may simply be that, unlike brick or glass, there is a natural equivalent. For this reason, the artificial stone material is nearly always seen as a second choice, only to be used if one cannot afford the real thing. Sadly, this takes no account of the impressive physical properties of the material, which are at least the equal of carved stone. It also takes no account of the artistic and technical capabilities of the artisans involved in the artificial stone industry who are, through their modelling and mould-making skills, often able to create designs with details far exceeding the capabilities of the average stone mason. Whilst the current generation applauds the skills of the craftsmen at Coade, for example, they were derided by many of their contemporaries. Their successors in the twenty-first century often experience the same problems and prejudices even though, through technological advances and rigorous testing regimes, the quality of artificial stone from a United Kingdom Cast Stone Association member is undoubtedly higher and more consistent than has been created at any time in the history of artificial stone. One can only wonder how historians will review the works of present day manufacturers in the centuries to come, for it would appear that it is only with hindsight that we are prepared to properly judge this material.

Endnotes

1............John Davis, *Antique Garden Ornament* (Woodbridge, 1991), p. 161.
2............Susan Dawson, *Cast in Concrete* (London, 1995), p. 3.
3............Batty Langley, *New Principles of Gardening* (London, 1728), p. 203.
4............Gervase Jackson-Stops (ed.), *The Treasure Houses of Britain* (New Haven & London, 1985), p. 126.
5............Jeremy Black, *Italy and the Grand Tour* (New Haven & London, 2003), p. 194.
6............Francis Haskell and Nicholas Penny, *Taste and the Antique* (New Haven & London, 1981), p. 85.
7............Haskell and Penny, *Taste and the Antique*, pp. 96-98.
8............Chris Stanley and Gillian Bond, *Concrete through the Ages* (Crowthorne, 1999), p. 2.
9............Dawson, *Cast in Concrete*, p. 27.
10..........John Claudius Loudon, *Encyclopaedia of Cottage, Farm, and Villa Architecture and Furniture* (London, 1846), p. 142.
11..........Jim Keeling, *The Terracotta Gardener* (London, 1990), p. 24.
12..........Hans van Lemmen, *Coade Stone* (Princes Risborough, 2006), p. 8.
13..........Davis, *Antique Garden Ornament*, pp. 161-162.
14..........John Ruch, 'Regency Coade: a Study of the Coade Record Books, 1813-21' in J. Mordaunt Crook (ed.), *Architectural History*, Vol. 11 (1968), p. 44.
15..........Astragal, 'The Secret's Out', *Architects' Journal*, Vol. 191, No. 24 (13 June 1990), p. 6.
16..........Samuel Ireland, *Picturesque Views on the River Thames from its Source in Gloucestershire to the Nore* (London, 1799), p. 192.
17..........Lemmen, *Coade Stone*, p. 9.
18..........Ireland, *Picturesque Views on the River Thames*, p. 192.
19..........Alison Kelly, *Mrs Coade's Stone* (Upton-upon-Severn, 1990), p. 62.
20..........Llewellynn Jewitt, *The Ceramic Art of Great Britain* (London, 1878), p. 140.
21..........Ruch, 'Coade Record Books', *Architectural History*, p. 50.
22..........Alison Kelly, 'Mrs Coade's Stone', *Museum of Garden History*, Journal 9 (Autumn 2003), p. 15.
23..........Ruch, 'Coade Record Books', *Architectural History*, p. 55.
24..........Kelly, 'Mrs Coade's Stone', *Museum of Garden History*, pp. 14-15.
25..........Alison Kelly, 'Eleanor Coade', *Oxford Dictionary of National Biography*, www.oxforddnb.com/view/printable/37296 (accessed 19 October 2007).
26..........Lemmen, *Coade Stone*, pp. 12-13.
27..........Blashfield, John Marriott, *An Account of the History and Manufacture of Ancient and Modern Terra Cotta* (London, 1855), pp. 25-27.
28..........John Summerson, *Architecture in Britain 1530-1830* (New Haven & London, 1993), p. 439.
29..........Robert Kerr, 'On Artificial Stone', *RIBA Transactions 1862-63* (London,1863), p. 145.
30..........British Standards Institute, *Specification for Cast Stone BS 1217: 1997* (London, 1997), p. 1.
31..........Dawson, *Cast in Concrete*, p. 6.
32..........Dawson, *Cast in Concrete*, p. 6.
33..........Dawson, *Cast in Concrete*, p. 6.
34..........Louisa Smith, 'Cast Stone: a Genuine Alternative', *Listed Heritage* (September/October 2007), p. 50.
35..........Davis, *Antique Garden Ornament*, pp. 193-194.
36..........Tally Wade, 'Haddonstone Cast-Limestone Factory', *AJ Specification* (February 2008), p. 12.
37..........Linda Jewell, 'Cast Stone', *Landscape Architecture*, Vol. 76, No. 5 (September/October 1986), p. 122.
38..........Paul Edwards, *English Garden Ornament* (Cranbury, New Jersey, 1965), p. 68.
39..........Bennet Woodcroft, *Subject-matter Index (made from titles only) of Patents of Invention, from March 2, 1617 (14 James I) to October 1, 1852 (16 Victoria)* (London, 1857), pp. 786-787.
40..........Patent of Thomas Ripley and Richard Holt, 'Compound Metal for Manufacturing Artificial Stone and Marble', Number 447, *British Library* (London, 1722).
41..........Lesley Brown (ed.), *Shorter Oxford English Dictionary* (Oxford, 2002), p. 1758.
42..........Richard Holt, *A Short Treatise of Artificial Stone* (London, 1730).
43..........Holt, *Treatise of Artificial Stone*, p. 13.
44..........Holt, *Treatise of Artificial Stone*, pp. 16-17.

45..........Holt, *Treatise of Artificial Stone*, p. 40.
46..........Katherine Esdaile, 'Coade Stone', *The Architect & Building News* (19 January 1940), p. 95.
47..........Esdaile,'Coade Stone', *The Architect & Building News*, p. 95.
48..........Lemmen, *Coade Stone*, p. 8.
49..........Daniel Pincot, *An Essay on the Origin, Nature, Uses, and Properties, of Artificial Stone* (London, 1770), p. 47.
50..........Patricia Scott, *Pottery in Lambeth – a Select Bibliography* (Lambeth, 1976), p. 1.
51..........Eileen Harris, *British Architectural Books and Writers 1556-1785* (Cambridge, 1990), p. 237.
52..........Pincot, *Artificial Stone*, p. 47.
53..........Esdaile,'Coade Stone', *The Architect & Building News*, p. 95.
54..........Jennie Cupial, 'The Coades and their Stone', *Concrete*, Vol. 14, No. 10 (October 1980), p. 19.
55..........Kelly, *Mrs Coade's Stone*, p. 32.
56..........Pincot, *Artificial Stone*, p. 47.
57..........Kelly, *Mrs Coade's Stone*, p. 32.
58..........Harris, *British Architectural Books and Writers*, p. 263.
59..........Harris, *British Architectural Books and Writers*, p. 265.
60..........Esdaile,'Coade Stone', *The Architect & Building News*, p. 95.
61..........George Vertue, *Notebooks III*, June 1731, BL Add MS 23.076, fol. 33. p. 51.
62..........Horace Walpole, *Anecdotes of Painting in England* (London, 1798), p. 485.
63..........Howard Colvin, *A Biographical Dictionary of British Architects 1600-1840* (New Haven & London, 1995), p. 597.
64..........Kelly, *Mrs Coade's Stone*, p. 32.
65..........Davis, *Antique Garden Ornament*, p. 159.
66..........John Gwynn, *London and Westminster Improved* (London, 1766), pp. 82-83.
67..........*Public Advertiser*, 10 February 1767.
68..........Harris, *British Architectural Books and Writers*, p. 371.
69..........Kelly, *Mrs Coade's Stone*, p. 33.
70..........Harris, *British Architectural Books and Writers*, p. 371.
71..........Summerson, *Architecture in Britain*, p. 439.
72..........Kelly, 'Eleanor Coade', *Oxford Dictionary of National Biography*.
73..........Rupert Gunnis, *Dictionary of British Sculptors 1660-1851* (London, 1964), p. 105.
74..........Kelly, *Mrs Coade's Stone*, p. 200.
75..........Coade, *A Descriptive Catalogue of Coade's Artificial Stone Manufactory* (London, 1784).
76..........Harris, *British Architectural Books and Writers*, p. 372
77..........Jewitt, *Ceramic Art of Great Britain*, p. 141.
78..........Jewitt, *Ceramic Art of Great Britain*, p. 142.
79..........Esdaile,'Coade Stone', *The Architect & Building News*, p. 95.
80..........Kelly, 'Eleanor Coade', *Oxford Dictionary of National Biography*.
81..........Kelly, 'Mrs Coade's Stone', *Museum of Garden History*, p. 13.
82..........Lemmen, *Coade Stone*, p. 5.
83..........Kelly, 'Mrs Coade's Stone', *Museum of Garden History*, p. 14.
84..........Mary Ann Steggles, 'John Bacon', *Oxford Dictionary of National Biography*, www.oxforddnb.com/articles/0/994-article.html?back=,37296 (accessed 19 October 2007).
85..........Robert Bisset, *The Historical, Biographical, Literary, and Scientific Magazine. The History of Europe, for the Year 1799. With an Obituary and Biographical Sketches of Persons Deceased in that Year, &c.* (London, c1800), p. 81.
86..........James Edward Holroyd, 'Well-kept Secret of Coade Stone', *The Times* (5 March 1966), p. 9.
87..........Kelly, 'Eleanor Coade', *Oxford Dictionary of National Biography*.
88..........Lemmen, *Coade Stone*, p. 20.
89..........Kelly, 'Eleanor Coade', *Oxford Dictionary of National Biography*.
90..........Kelly, *Mrs Coade's Stone*, pp. 319-330.
91..........Coade, *Etchings of Coade's Artificial Stone Manufactory* (London, c1779).
92..........Coade, *A Descriptive Catalogue*, p. 1.
93..........Kelly, *Mrs Coade's Stone*, p. 92.
94..........Kelly, *Mrs Coade's Stone*, pp. 92-93.
95..........Gunnis, *Dictionary of British Sculptors*, p. 106.
96..........Gunnis, *Dictionary of British Sculptors*, p. 106.
97..........Davis, *Antique Garden Ornament*, p. 164.
98..........Anon., *The History and Antiquities of the Parish of Lambeth* (London, 1786), pp. 82-83.
99..........Ireland, *Picturesque Views on the River Thames*, p. 192.
100........Lemmen, *Coade Stone*, p. 5.
101........Kelly, *Mrs Coade's Stone*, p. 41.

102........Kelly, *Mrs Coade's Stone*, p. 43.
103........Ruch, 'Coade Record Books', *Architectural History*, p. 45.
104........Ruch, 'Coade Record Books', *Architectural History*, p. 34.
105........Kelly, 'Eleanor Coade', *Oxford Dictionary of National Biography*.
106........Michael Symes, *A Glossary of Garden History* (Princes Risborough, 1993), p. 34.
107........Davis, *Antique Garden Ornament*, p. 167.
108........Davis, *Antique Garden Ornament*, p. 167.
109........Kelly, *Mrs Coade's Stone*, p. 60.
110........Kelly, 'Eleanor Coade', Oxford *Dictionary of National Biography* and Lemmen, *Coade Stone*, p. 19.
111........Julia Abel-Smith, 'The Umbrello at Great Saxham, Suffolk', *The Georgian Group Report and Journal 1987* (Lavenham, 1988), p. 77.
112........Abel-Smith, 'Umbrello at Great Saxham', *Georgian Group Report*, p. 84.
113........Ruch, 'Coade Record Books', *Architectural History*, p. 39.
114........Hans van Lemmen, 'Ceramic Follies' in Susan Kellerman (ed.), *The Follies Journal*, No. 7 (Winter 2007), p. 23.
115........Ruch, 'Coade Record Books', *Architectural History*, p. 40.
116........Kelly, *Mrs Coade's Stone*, p. 74.
117........Lemmen, *Coade Stone*, p. 7.
118........Esdaile,'Coade Stone', *The Architect & Building News*, p. 94.
119........Dawson, *Cast in Concrete*, p. 27.
120........Coade, *Description of Ornamental Stone in the Gallery of Coade and Sealy* (London, 1799).
121........Lemmen, *Coade Stone*, p. 6.
122........Ruch, 'Coade Record Books', *Architectural History*, p. 36.
123........Gunnis, *Dictionary of British Sculptors*, p. 346.
124........Kelly, *Mrs Coade's Stone*, p. 49.
125........Ruch, 'Coade Record Books', *Architectural History*, p. 46.
126........Croggon's Day Book, Order Book and Letter Book, *National Archives*, C111/106.
127........Ruch, 'Coade Record Books', *Architectural History*.
128........Ruch, 'Coade Record Books', *Architectural History*, p. 35.
129........Ruch, 'Coade Record Books', *Architectural History*, p. 35.
130........Gunnis, *Dictionary of British Sculptors*, p. 116
131........Ruch, 'Coade Record Books', *Architectural History*, p. 36.
132........Ruch, 'Coade Record Books', *Architectural History*, p. 40.
133........Kelly, *Mrs Coade's Stone*, pp. 301-302
134........Davis, *Antique Garden Ornament*, p. 165.
135........Kelly, *Mrs Coade's Stone*, p. 50.
136........Ruch, 'Coade Record Books', *Architectural History*, p. 36.
137........Anon., 'Coade's Artificial Stone Works', *British History Online*, www.british-history.ac.uk/ report.aspx?compid=47044&strquery=Coade (accessed 5 June 2007).
138........Kelly, *Mrs Coade's Stone*, p. 50.
139........Jewitt, *Ceramic Art of Great Britain*, p. 139.
140........Anon., The Art Journal Illustrated Catalogue: *The Industry of all Nations* (London, 1851), p. 70.
141........Davis, *Antique Garden Ornament*, pp. 160-161.
142........Barbara Israel, *Antique Garden Ornament* (New York, 1999), p. 43.
143........Gunnis, *Dictionary of British Sculptors*, p. 56.
144........Richard Funnell, *Nineteenth Century Artificial Stone Garden Vases and Plant Containers* (London, 1997), p. 41.
145........Jewitt, *Ceramic Art of Great Britain*, p. 153.
146........Jewitt, *Ceramic Art of Great Britain*, p. 153.
147........Funnell, *Nineteenth Century Artificial Stone*, p. 41.
148........Rupert van der Werff and Jackie Rees, *Garden Antiques* (London, 2003), p. 84.
149........Israel, *Antique Garden Ornament*, p. 166.
150........Jewitt, *Ceramic Art of Great Britain*, p. 153.
151........Gunnis, *Dictionary of British Sculptors*, p. 56.
152........Haskell and Penny, *Taste and the Antique*, p. 122.
153........Wyatt, Parker & Co., *Figures, Vases, Fountains &c.* (London, 1841).
154........Blashfield, *Ancient and Modern Terra Cotta*, p. 20.
155........John Smith, 'John Marriott Blashfield', *Oxford Dictionary of National Biography*, *www.oxforddnb.com/view/ printable/49435* (accessed 19 October 2007).
156........Davis, *Antique Garden Ornament*, p. 178.
157........John Marriott Blashfield, *A Selection of Vases, Statues, Busts, &c. from Terra-Cottas* (London, 1857), p. 1.

158........Jewitt, *The Ceramic Art of Great Britain*, p. 435.
159........John Smith, David Heeley and James Heeson, *Blashfield's – the History, Suggested Guidelines and Ideas for its Regeneration* (Stamford, 2000), p. i.
160........Smith, Heeley & Heeson, *Blashfield's*, pp. i-ii.
161........Gunnis, *Dictionary of British Sculptors*, p. 56.
162........Smith, 'John Marriott Blashfield', *Oxford Dictionary of National Biography*.
163........Davis, *Antique Garden Ornament*, pp. 179-180.
164........Jewitt, *The Ceramic Art of Great Britain*, p. 437.
165........John Smith, 'Blashfield Lecture 1984', *Stamford Museum Archives* (unpublished 1984), p. 5.
166........Smith, 'John Marriott Blashfield', *Oxford Dictionary of National Biography*.
167........Smith, 'John Marriott Blashfield', *Oxford Dictionary of National Biography*.
168........Smith, 'John Marriott Blashfield', *Oxford Dictionary of National Biography*.
169........Gunnis, *Dictionary of British Sculptors*, p. 408.
170........Gunnis, *Dictionary of British Sculptors*, p. 22.
171........Ruch, 'Coade Record Books', *Architectural History*, p. 35.
172........Miles Hadfield, 'Letters', *Country Life* (11 February 1960), p. 280.
173........Funnell, *Nineteenth Century Artificial Stone*, p. 21.
174........Felix Austin, *Collection of Ornaments at Austin's Artificial Stone Works* (London, 1838), p. 2.
175........Austin, *Collection of Ornaments*, p. 2.
176........Austin, *Collection of Ornaments*, p. 2.
177........Gunnis, *Dictionary of British Sculptors*, p. 22.
178........Davis, *Antique Garden Ornament*, pp. 201-202.
179........Israel, *Antique Garden Ornament*, p. 216.
180........Kerr, 'On Artificial Stone', *RIBA Transactions 1862-63*, p. 144.
181........Davis, *Antique Garden Ornament*, p. 205.
182........Davis, *Antique Garden Ornament*, p. 199.
183........Austin & Seeley, 'Advertisement', *The Gardeners' Chronicle and Agricultural Gazette* (13 January 1872), p. 37.
184........Funnell, *Nineteenth Century Artificial Stone*, p. 47.
185........Desmond Eyles, (ed.), *Sir Henry Doulton* (London, 1970), p. 2.
186........Eyles, (ed.), *Sir Henry Doulton*, p. 21.
187........Jewitt, *The Ceramic Art of Great Britain*, p. 145.
188........Davis, *Antique Garden Ornament*, p. 209.
189........Desmond Eyles, *The Doulton Lambeth Wares* (London, 1975), p. 163.
190........Jewitt, *The Ceramic Art of Great Britain*, p. 148.
191........Davis, *Antique Garden Ornament*, p. 217.
192........Jewitt, *The Ceramic Art of Great Britain*, p. 148.
193........George Plumtre, *Garden Ornament* (London, 1989), p. 237.
194........Davis, *Antique Garden Ornament*, p. 210.
195........Paul Atterbury and Louise Irvine, *The Doulton Story* (London, 1979), p. 68.
196........Davis, *Antique Garden Ornament*, p. 211.
197........Davis, *Antique Garden Ornament*, p. 217.
198........Atterbury and Irvine, *The Doulton Story*, p. 69.
199........Davis, *Antique Garden Ornament*, p. 210.
200........Camilla Beresford and David Mason, *Durability Guaranteed* (Swindon, 2007), p. 7.
201........Kate Banister, 'The Pulham Family of Hertfordshire and their Work' in Anne Rowe (ed.), *Hertfordshire Garden History* (Hatfield, 2007), p. 137.
202........Gunnis, *Dictionary of British Sculptors*, p. 312.
203........Davis, *Antique Garden Ornament*, p. 186.
204........Banister, 'The Pulham Family' in Rowe (ed.), *Hertfordshire Garden History*, p. 137.
205........Beresford and Mason, *Durability Guaranteed*, p. 4.
206........Beresford and Mason, *Durability Guaranteed*, p. 3.
207........James Pulham, *Picturesque Rock Garden Scenery, &c.* (London, c1877), p. 47.
208........Jewitt, *The Ceramic Art of Great Britain*, p. 431.
209........Davis, *Antique Garden Ornament*, p. 192.
210........Jewitt, *The Ceramic Art of Great Britain*, p. 429.
211........James Pulham, *Garden Ornament* (London, c1925), p. 76.
212........Jewitt, *The Ceramic Art of Great Britain*, p. 428.
213........Pulham, *Picturesque Rock Garden Scenery*, p. 47.
214........Pulham, *Picturesque Rock Garden Scenery*, p. 81.

215........Davis, *Antique Garden Ornament*, pp. 191-192.
216........Pulham, *Garden Ornament*, p. 2.
217........Pulham & Son, 'Advertisement', *The Times* (26 February 1927), p. 6.
218........Banister, 'The Pulham Family' in Rowe (ed.), *Hertfordshire Garden History*, p. 143.
219........Ralph Davison, *Concrete Pottery and Garden Furniture* (New York, 1917), p. iii.
220........Ibstock Hathernware, 'Products', *www.hathernware.co.uk/products/products-frame.htm* (accessed 19 September 2007).
221........Funnell, *Nineteenth Century Artificial Stone*, pp. 72-74.
222........Graham Rose, *The Traditional Garden Book* (London, 1989), p. 182.
223........Inès Heugel, *Classic Garden Style* (New York, 2004), p. 23.
224........Gaynor Gilbert, Chilstone, email dated 5 February 2008.
225........Gaynor Gilbert , Chilstone, interview 31 August 2007.
226........Gilbert, email dated 5 February 2008.
227........Mammon, 'How to Urn a Living', *The Observer*, 24 October 1971, p. 25.
228........Gilbert , interview 31 August 2007.
229........Robert Barrow, Diaries, *Haddonstone Archives*, 1972-1990.
230........Gilbert, email dated 5 February 2008..
231........Gaynor Gilbert, Chilstone, email dated 25 February 2008.
232........Hesway Limited, 'Creditsafe Online Credit Report', *www1.creditsafeuk.com* (accessed 20 August 2007).
233........Steptrack Limited, 'Creditsafe Online Credit Report', *www1.creditsafeuk.com* (accessed 5 February 2008).
234........Hesway Limited, 'Creditsafe Online Credit Report', *www1.creditsafeuk.com* (accessed 5 February 2008).
235........Chilstone, 'Material Specification', *www.Chilstone.com/Info_Sheets/Tech6_Material%20Specification.htm* (accessed 5 February 2008).
236........Anon., *Financial Times*, (15 August 1970).
237........Anthony Huxley (ed.), *Chilstone 1972-1973* (Newport Pagnell, c1974).
238........David Barrow, 'Why Haddonstone? The Early Years', *Haddonstone Archives*, (unpublished 2007).
239........Barrow, Diaries.
240........Barrow, 'Why Haddonstone?'
241........Mammon, 'How to Urn a Living', *The Observer*, p. 25.
242........Barrow, 'Why Haddonstone?'
243........Royal Horticultural Society, *Catalogue of Chelsea Show 1972* (Rochester, 1972), p. 38.
244........Haddonstone Archives: 1971 to present, *Haddonstone*, uncatalogued.
245........Iudex Limited, Report and Accounts, *Haddonstone Archives*, 31 July 1973.
246........James Barrow, Haddonstone Public Relations 1987, *Haddonstone Archives*, 28 May 1986 – 3 December 1987.
247........Barrow, 'Why Haddonstone?'
248........Barrow, Diaries.
249........Iudex, Report and Accounts.
250........Haddonstone, *catalogue and price list*, autumn 1972.
251........Haddonstone, *catalogue and price list*, autumn 1972.
252........Haddonstone, *UK price list*, 1 January 2009.
253........Iudex, Report and Accounts
254........Barrow, Diaries.
255........Barrow, Haddonstone Public Relations, 1987.
256........Lucinda Lambton, Beastly Buildings (London, 1985), p. 86.
257........Barrow, Haddonstone Public Relations, 1987.
258........Barrow, Haddonstone Public Relations, 1987.
259........Barrow, Haddonstone Public Relations, 1987.
260........James Barrow, letter to Mr C Howarth of Stevenage, *Haddonstone Archives*, 28 May 1986.
261........Neil Sparrow, 'Haddonstone Architectural Sales History', *Haddonstone Archives*, information provided 15 February 2008.
262........Haddonstone, Board Notes 1987- present, *Haddonstone Archives*.
263........Simon Scott (ed.), *Haddonstone News*, Number 8 (December 1996).
264........Scott (ed.), *Haddonstone News*, Number 9 (March 1997).
265........Scott (ed.), *Haddonstone News*, Number 40 (Christmas 2004).
266........Scott (ed.), *Haddonstone News*, Number 50 (Spring 2008).
267........Scott (ed.), *Haddonstone News*, Number 45 (Christmas 2006).
268........Smith, 'Cast Stone', *Listed Heritage* (September/October 2007), p. 50.
269........Israel, *Antique Garden Ornament*, p. 50.
270........Israel, *Antique Garden Ornament*, p. 63.

271........Haskell and Penny, *Taste and the Antique*, p. 315.

272........Smith, 'Cast Stone', *Listed Heritage* (September/October 2007), p. 50.

273........Rob Cassy, *Garden UK* (London 2003), p. 154.

274........Cassy, *Garden UK*, p. 154.

275........Charles Wagner and Ian McCaig, 'Cast Stone', *Traditional Homes* (October 1987), p. 16.

276........Holt, *Treatise of Artificial Stone*, p. vii.

277........Holt, *Treatise of Artificial Stone*, p. 6.

278........Holt, *Treatise of Artificial Stone*, pp. 7-8.

279........Patent of Ripley and Holt, 'Compound Metal', Number 447.

280........Pincot, *Artificial Stone*, p. 4.

281........Pincot, *Artificial Stone*, p. 6.

282........Pincot, *Artificial Stone*, p. 74.

283........Pincot, *Artificial Stone*, pp. 77-78.

284........Anon., *Times* (3 September 1785), p. 3.

285........Ruch, 'Coade Record Books', *Architectural History*, p. 43.

286........John Marriott Blashfield, 'Ancient and Modern Pottery', *Associated Architectural Societies Reports and Papers* (1859), p. 128.

287........Davis, *Antique Garden Ornament*, p. 164.

288........Summerson, *Architecture in Britain*, p. 439.

289........Rose, *Traditional Garden Book*, p. 173.

290........Kelly, *Mrs Coade's Stone*, p. 313.

291........William Shenstone, *The Works in Verse and Prose* (London, 1764), vol. II, p. 135.

292........Funnell, *Nineteenth Century Artificial Stone*, p. 11.

293........Blashfield, *Ancient and Modern Terra Cotta*, p. 12.

294........Smith, 'John Marriott Blashfield', *Oxford Dictionary of National Biography*.

295........Jewitt, *The Ceramic Art of Great Britain*, p. 428.

296........Atterbury and Irvine, *Doulton Story*, pp. 68-69.

297........Funnell, *Nineteenth Century Artificial Stone*, p. 43.

298........Wagner and McCaig, 'Cast Stone', *Traditional Homes*, p. 10.

299........Dawson, *Cast in Concrete*, p. 30.

300........Jill Billington, *New Classic Gardens* (London, 2000), p. 22.

301........Frederick Chatterton (ed.), 'Cast Stone', *Specification*, No. 28 (1926), p. 11.

302........F.R.S. Yorke, 'Concrete and Artificial Stone', *Architects' Journal* (1 June 1932), p. 729.

303........Charles Holden, 'Memo dated 15 June 1942', Adams Holden + Pearson Papers 1894-1992, *RIBA Archives*, Box 26, AHP/26/17/1.

304........Giles Worsley, 'Is Architecture Going Back to the Sixties?', *Daily Telegraph Arts & Books* (11 November 2000), p. 11.

305........Wagner and Ian McCaig, 'Cast Stone', *Traditional Homes*, p. 10.

306........Wagner and Ian McCaig, 'Cast Stone', *Traditional Homes*, p. 12.

307........Theodore Prudon, 'Simulating Stone, 1860-1940', *The Journal of Preservation Technology*, Vol. XXI, Nos. 3/4 (1989), p. 79.

308........Ulrich Conrads (ed.), *Programmes and Manifestoes on 20th-century Architecture* (London, 1970), pp. 20-22.

309........Conrads (ed.), *Programmes and Manifestoes*, p. 36.

310........Conrads (ed.), *Programmes and Manifestoes*, p. 109.

311........Conrads (ed.), *Programmes and Manifestoes*, p. 100.

312........Horace Walpole, *The History of the Modern Taste in Gardening* (New York, 1995), p. 26.

313........Charles Jencks and Karl Kropf (eds.), *Theories and Manifestoes of Contemporary Architecture* (Chichester, 1997), p. 9.

314........Jencks and Kropf (eds.), *Theories and Manifestoes*, p. 182.

315........Jencks and Kropf (eds.), *Theories and Manifestoes*, p. 201.

316........Jencks and Kropf (eds.), *Theories and Manifestoes*, pp. 205-206.

317........HRH The Prince of Wales, *A Vision of Britain* (London, 1989), p. 91.

318........Anon., 'Artificial Stone Rejected for Extension', *Planning* (19 October 2007), p. 21.

319........Davis, *Antique Garden Ornament*, p. 161.

320........David Hicks, *Garden Design* (London, 1982), p. 148.

321........James Bartholomew, *Yew & Non-Yew* (London, 1996), pp. 12-13.

322........Bartholomew, *Yew & Non-Yew*, p. 111

323........Werff and Rees, *Garden Antiques*, p. 7.

324........Werff and Rees, *Garden Antiques*, p. 19.

325........Rowland, Tom, 'Nice Little Urns Grow Money for Owners', *The Daily Telegraph* (11 May 1992), p. 4.

326........Werff and Rees, *Garden Antiques*, p. 82.

327........Davis, *Antique Garden Ornament*, p. 127.
328........Davis, *Antique Garden Ornament*, p. 128.
329........Blashfield, *Account of the History and Manufacture*, p. 15.
330........David Jefferson, Seamus Hanna and Bill Martin, *Identifying and Sourcing Stone for Historic Building Repair* (Swindon, 2006), p. 2.
331........Paul Drury and Anna McPherson, *Conservation Principles, Second Stage Consultation* (London, 2007), p. 26.
332........Drury and McPherson, *Conservation Principles*, p. 37.
333........Drury and McPherson, *Conservation Principles*, p. 46.
334........Drury and McPherson, *Conservation Principles*, p. 42.
335........Drury and McPherson, *Conservation Principles*, p. 60.
336........Richard Carr, 'Set in their Ways', *Building Design* (26 October 1990), p. 33.
337........United Kingdom Cast Stone Association, *Research Study into the Development of a Standard Test Method and Performance Specification for Cast Stone* (Crowthorne, 2000), p. 1.
338........Christopher Gallagher, National Trust Curator (Gardens & Parks) North Territory, telephone conversation 11 December 2007 and Julian Gibbs, National Trust Curator (Gardens & Parks) West Territory, telephone conversation 17 December 2007.
339........Jenifer White, English Heritage Senior Landscape Advisor, email dated 12 November 2007.
340........John Stewart, English Heritage Building Conservation & Research, email dated 13 November 2007.
341........Wagner and McCaig, 'Cast Stone', *Traditional Homes*, p. 20.
342........Diane Green, Inspector of Historic Buildings, English Heritage Yorkshire Region, letter to Katherine Sycamore of Yorkshire Dales National Park Authority, 31 August 2005.
343........Mark Stephenson, Mark, Building Conservation Officer, Yorkshire Dales National Park Authority, memorandum to Katherine Sycamore of Yorkshire Dales National Park Authority, dated 19 January 2006.
344........Anon., *Hints for City Amusements; or, Bank Oratory Anticipated* (London, 1788), p. 23.
345........Davis, *Antique Garden Ornament*, p. 111.
346........John Wood, *An Essay Towards a Description of Bath* (London, 1749), p. 426.
347........Kerr, 'On Artificial Stone', *RIBA Transactions 1862-63*, p. 142.
348........Blashfield, *Vases, Statues, Busts, &c.*, pp. 2-3.
349........Plumtre, *Garden Ornament*, p. 218.
350........Pincot, *Artificial Stone*, p. 11.
351........Pincot, *Artificial Stone*, p. 35.
352........John Fidler, 'Stone from the Mould', *Traditional Homes* (May 1992), p. 65.
353........Chatterton, 'Cast Stone', *Specification*, p. 13.
354........Astragal, 'The Secret's Out', *Architects' Journal*, p. 6.
355........Pincot, *Artificial Stone*, p. 46.
356........Richard Smith, letter dated 21 May 2009.
357........Richard Smith, letter dated 22 June 2009.
358........Smith, letter dated 21 May 2009.
359........Smith, letter dated 21 May 2009.
360........Alison Kelly, 'Sir John Soane and Mrs Eleanor Coade', *Apollo* (April 1989), p. 247.
361........Prince of Wales, Vision of Britain, p. 10.
362........Iovine, Julie, 'A Discreet Ornamentalism', *New York Times*, *http://query.nytimes.com/gst/fullpage.html?res–9E06E2DE153DF935A35753C1A96* (accessed 1 May 2008).
363........Davis, *Antique Garden Ornament*, p. 71.
364........Ada-Louise Huxtable, 'Historical Survey', *Progressive Architecture 41* (October 1960), p. 88.
365........Gerhard Auer, 'Magic of Materials', *Daidalos 56* (Juni 1995), p. 20.
366........Pincot, *Artificial Stone*, p. 78.

Bibliography

Primary Sources

Barrow, David, 'Why Haddonstone? The Early Years', *Haddonstone Archives*, (unpublished 2007).

Barrow, James, letter to Mr C Howarth of Stevenage, *Haddonstone Archives*, 28 May 1986.

Barrow, James, Haddonstone Public Relations 1987, *Haddonstone Archives*, 28 May 1986 – 3 December 1987.

Barrow, Robert, Diaries, *Haddonstone Archives*, 1972-1990.

Croggon's Day Book, Order Book and Letter Book, *National Archives*, C111/106.

Davis, John, Archives, viewed 15 September 2007.

Davis, John, letter dated 24 September 2008.

Davis, John, 'Artificial Stone' lecture, *Museum of Garden History*, 8 December 2008.

Gallagher, Christopher, National Trust Curator (Gardens & Parks) North Territory, telephone conversation 11 December 2007.

Gibbs, Julian, National Trust Curator (Gardens & Parks) West Territory, telephone conversation 17 December 2007.

Gilbert, Gaynor, Chilstone, interview 31 August 2007.

Gilbert, Gaynor, Chilstone, email dated 5 February 2008.

Gilbert, Gaynor, Chilstone, email dated 25 February 2008.

Green, Diane, Inspector of Historic Buildings, English Heritage Yorkshire Region, letter to Katherine Sycamore of Yorkshire Dales National Park Authority, 31 August 2005.

Haddonstone Archives: 1971 to present, *Haddonstone*, uncatalogued.

Haddonstone Board Notes, *Haddonstone Archives*, 1987-present.

Haddonstone, Report and Accounts, *Haddonstone Archives*, 1973-present.

Holden, Charles, 'Memo dated 15 June 1942', Adams Holden + Pearson Papers 1894-1992, *RIBA Archives*, Box 26, AHP/26/17/1.

Iudex Limited, Report and Accounts, *Haddonstone Archives*, 31 July 1973.

Lloyd's Evening Post, 18-21 December 1767.

Patent of Thomas Ripley and Richard Holt, 'Compound Metal for Manufacturing Artificial Stone and Marble', Number 447, *British Library* (London, 1722).

Public Advertiser, 10 February 1767.

Smith, John, 'Blashfield Lecture 1984', *Stamford Museum Archives* (unpublished 1984).

Smith, Richard, letter dated 21 May 2009.

Smith, Richard, letter dated 22 June 2009.

Sparrow, Neil, 'Haddonstone Architectural Sales History', *Haddonstone Archives*, information provided 15 February 2008.

Stephenson, Mark, Building Conservation Officer, Yorkshire Dales National Park Authority, memorandum to Katherine Sycamore of Yorkshire Dales National Park Authority, dated 19 January 2006.

Stewart, John, English Heritage Building Conservation & Research, email dated 13 November 2007.

Vertue, George, *Notebooks III*, June 1731, BL Add MS 23.076, fol. 33.

White, Jenifer, English Heritage Senior Landscape Advisor, email dated 12 November 2007.

Secondary Sources

Abel-Smith, Julia, 'The Umbrello at Great Saxham, Suffolk', *The Georgian Group Report and Journal 1987* (Lavenham, 1988), pp. 77-87.

Anon., Times (3 September 1785), p. 3.

Anon., *The History and Antiquities of the Parish of Lambeth* (London, 1786).

Anon., *Hints for City Amusements; or, Bank Oratory Anticipated* (London, 1788).

Anon., *Ambulator; or, a Pocket Companion in a Tour Round London* (London, 1793).

Anon., *The Art Journal Illustrated Catalogue: The Industry of all Nations* (London, 1851).

Anon., Financial Times (15 August 1970).

Anon., 'Artificial Stone Rejected for Extension', *Planning* (19 October 2007), p. 21.

Astragal, 'The Secret's Out', *Architects' Journal*, Vol. 191, No. 24 (13 June 1990), pp. 6-7.

Atterbury, Paul, 'Doulton in the Garden', *Country Life* (4 September 1980), p. 810.

Atterbury, Paul and Louise Irvine, *The Doulton Story* (London, 1979).

Auer, Gerhard, 'Magic of Materials', *Daidalos 56* (Juni 1995), pp. 19-20.

Austin, Felix, *Collection of Ornaments at Austin's Artificial Stone Works* (London, 1838).

Austin & Seeley, 'Advertisement', *The Gardeners' Chronicle and Agricultural Gazette* (13 January 1872), p. 37.

Baistow, Diane, 'Weathering Well', *The English Garden* (March 2004), pp. 62-64.

Banister, Kate, 'The Pulham Family of Hertfordshire and their Work' in Anne Rowe (ed.), *Hertfordshire Garden History* (Hatfield, 2007), pp. 134-154.

Barry, James, *A Letter to the Dilettanti Society* (London, 1799).

Bartholomew, James, *Yew & Non-Yew* (London, 1996).

Bay, Philip de and James Bolton, *Garden Mania* (London, 2000).

Beadle, Dave, 'Reconstituted Stone: Casting about for a Replacement', *Building Trades Journal* (27 October 1983), p. 24.

Bell, Stanley, 'Star Cast', *Concrete Quarterly* (Winter 1991), pp. 10-12.

Beresford, Camilla and David Mason, *Durability Guaranteed* (Swindon, 2007).

Betjeman, John, *Ghastly Good Taste* (London, 1933).

Billington, Jill, *New Classic Gardens* (London, 2000).

Bisset, Robert, *The Historical, Biographical, Literary, and Scientific Magazine. The History of Europe, for the Year 1799. With an Obituary and Biographical Sketches of Persons Deceased in that Year, &c* (London, c1800).

Black, Jeremy, *The Grand Tour in the Eighteenth Century* (London, 1999).

Black, Jeremy, *Italy and the Grand Tour* (New Haven & London, 2003).

Blashfield, John Marriott, *An Account of the History and Manufacture of Ancient and Modern Terra Cotta* (London, 1855).

Blashfield, John Marriott, *Examples of Vases, Tazzas, Paterae, &c.* (London, 1855).

Blashfield, John Marriott, *A Catalogue of Five Hundred Articles Made of Patent Terra Cotta* (London, 1857).

Blashfield, John Marriott, *A Selection of Vases, Statues, Busts, &c. from Terra-Cottas* (London,1857).

Blashfield, John Marriott, *Terra-cotta Vases, Tazzae, figures, &c.* (London, c1857).

Blashfield, John Marriott, 'Ancient and Modern Pottery', *Associated Architectural Societies Reports and Papers* (1859), pp. 127-134.

Blashfield, John Marriott, *Domestic Architecture* (London, 1868).

Bolton, Arthur T., *The Architecture of Robert and James Adam, Volumes I & II* (Woodbridge, 1984).

British Standards Institute, *Specification for Cast Stone BS 1217: 1997* (London, 1997).

Brown, Lesley (ed.), *Shorter Oxford English Dictionary* (Oxford, 2002).

Carr, Richard, 'Set in their Ways', *Building Design* (26 October 1990), pp. 32-33.

Cassy, Rob, *Garden UK* (London, 2003).

Chatterton, Frederick (ed.), 'Cast Stone', *Specification*, No. 28 (1926), pp. 11-18.

Chilstone, catalogue and price list, spring 1974.

Chilstone, Architectural Stonework catalogue and price list, winter 2005/spring 2006.

Chilstone, Garden Ornaments catalogue and price list, spring/summer 2003.

Coade, *Etchings of Coade's Artificial Stone Manufactory* (London, c1779).

Coade, *A Descriptive Catalogue of Coade's Artificial Stone Manufactory* (London, 1784).

Coade, *Description of Ornamental Stone in the Gallery of Coade and Sealy* (London 1799).

Colvin, Howard, *A Biographical Dictionary of British Architects 1600-1840* (New Haven & London, 1995).

Conrads, Ulrich (ed.), *Programmes and Manifestoes on 20th-century Architecture* (London, 1970).

Crook, J Mordaunt, *The Greek Revival* (London, 1995).

Cupial, Jennie, 'The Coades and their Stone', *Concrete*, Vol. 14, No. 10 (October 1980), pp. 18-22.

Davis, John, *Antique Garden Ornament* (Woodbridge, 1991).

Davison, Ralph, *Concrete Pottery and Garden Furniture* (New York, 1917).

Dawson, Susan, *Cast in Concrete* (London,1995).

Dean, Ptolemy, *Sir John Soane and the Country Estate* (Aldershot & Vermont, 1999).

Doulton & Co., *Terra Cotta Garden Vases, Pedestals, Flower Pots and Every Other Description of Horticultural Terra Cotta* (London, 1893).

Doulton & Co., *Garden Ornaments by Doulton* (London, c1910).

Drury, Paul and Anna McPherson, *Conservation Principles*, Second Stage Consultation (London, 2007).

Dutton, Ralph, *The English Country House* (London, 1943-1944).

Edwards, Paul, *English Garden Ornament* (Cranbury, New Jersey, 1965).

Esdaile, Katherine, 'Coade Stone', *The Architect & Building News* (19 January 1940) pp. 94-96.

Esdaile, Katherine, 'Coade Stone', *The Architect & Building News* (26 January 1940) pp. 112-114.

Evelegh, Tessa, 'Going, Going, Gone!', *Practical Gardening* (June 1994), pp. 42-47.

Evers, Bernd (ed.), *Architectural Theory* (Cologne, 2006).

Eyles, Desmond (ed.), *Sir Henry Doulton* (London, 1970).

Eyles, Desmond, *The Doulton Lambeth Wares* (London, 1975).

Festing, Sally, 'Pulham Family Tree', *Garden History*, Vol 25 (1997), p231.

Fidler, John, 'Stone from the Mould', *Traditional Homes* (May 1992), pp. 65-68.

Floyd, Margaret Henderson, 'A Terra-Cotta Cornerstone for Copley Square', *Journal of the Society of Architectural Historians* (May 1973) pp. 88-102.

Funnell, Richard, *Nineteenth Century Artificial Stone Garden Vases and Plant Containers* (London,1997).

Gilbert, Gaynor and Kate Chitham (eds.), *Chilstone* (Tunbridge Wells, 1997).

Gillmore, QA, *A Practical Treatise on Coignet-Béton and Other Artificial Stone* (New York, 1871).

Girouard, Mark, *Life in the English Country House* (New Haven & London, 1978).

Gunnis, Rupert, *Dictionary of British Sculptors 1660-1851* (London, 1964).

Gwynn, John, *London and Westminster Improved* (London, 1766)

Haddonstone, *catalogue and price list*, autumn 1972.

Haddonstone, *catalogue*, March 2006.

Haddonstone, *UK price list*, 1 March 2008.

Hadfield, Miles, 'Letters', *Country Life* (11 February 1960), p. 280.

Hancock, A.E.R, 'Man's Reconstruction of Stone', *Building Materials* (November 1966) pp. 13-16.

Harris, Eileen, *British Architectural Books and Writers 1556-1785* (Cambridge, 1990).

Harris, John, *The Palladians* (London, 1981).

Harris, John, *The Palladian Revival* (New Haven & London, 1994).

Haskell, Francis and Nicholas Penny, *Taste and the Antique* (New Haven & London, 1981).

Heugel, Inès, *Classic Garden Style* (New York, 2004)

Hicks, David, *Garden Design* (London, 1982).

Holroyd, James Edward, 'Well-kept Secret of Coade Stone', *The Times* (5 March 1966), p. 9.

Holt, Richard, *A Short Treatise of Artificial Stone* (London, 1730).

Hunt, John Dixon and Peter Willis (eds.), *The Genius of the Place* (Cambridge, Massachusetts, 1988).

Hussey, Christopher, *English Country Houses, Early Georgian 1715-1760* (Woodbridge, 1986).

Hussey, Christopher (ed.), *English Country Houses, Mid Georgian 1760-1800* (Woodbridge, 1986).

Huxley, Anthony (ed.), *Chilstone 1972-1973* (Newport Pagnell, c1974).

Huxtable, Ada-Louise, 'Historical Survey', *Progressive Architecture 41* (October 1960), p.88.

Ireland, Samuel, *Picturesque Views on the River Thames from its Source in Gloucestershire to the Nore* (London, 1799).

Israel, Barbara, *Antique Garden Ornament* (New York, 1999).

Jackson-Stops, Gervase (ed.), *The Treasure Houses of Britain* (New Haven & London, 1985).

Jacques, David, *Georgian Gardens* (London, 1983).

Jefferson, David, Seamus Hanna and Bill Martin, *Identifying and Sourcing Stone for Historic Building Repair* (Swindon, 2006).

Jencks, Charles and Karl Kropf (eds.), *Theories and Manifestoes of Contemporary Architecture* (Chichester, 1997).

Jewell, Linda, 'Cast Stone', *Landscape Architecture*, Vol. 76, No. 5 (September/October 1986), pp. 122-125.

Jewitt, Llewellynn, *The Ceramic Art of Great Britain* (London, 1878).

Keeling, Jim, *The Terracotta Gardener* (London,1990).

Kelly, Alison, 'Sir John Soane and Mrs Eleanor Coade', *Apollo* (April 1989), pp. 247-253.

Kelly, Alison, *Mrs Coade's Stone* (Upton-upon-Severn, 1990).

Kelly, Alison, 'Mrs Coade's Stone', *Museum of Garden History*, Journal 9 (Autumn 2003), pp. 13-15.

Kerr, Robert, 'On Artificial Stone', *RIBA Transactions 1862-63* (London,1863).

Klein, Jack, 'Perfect Casting', *Architecture*, Vol. 87 No. 4 (April 1998), pp. 110-112.

Lambton, Lucinda, *Beastly Buildings* (London, 1985).

Langley, Batty, *New Principles of Gardening* (London, 1728).

Lees-Milne, James, *English Country Houses, Baroque 1685-1715* (Feltham, 1970).

Leigh, Samuel, *New Picture of London* (London, 1830).

Lemmen, Hans van, *Coade Stone* (Princes Risborough, 2006).

Lemmen, Hans van, 'Ceramic Follies' in Susan Kellerman (ed.), *The Follies Journal*, No. 7 (Winter 2007), pp. 23-40.

Lewis, Philippa, 'Cracking the Coade', *Period Living*, October 2008, p. 155.

Loriot, Antoine, *A Practical Essay, on a Cement and Artificial Stone, Justly Supposed to be that of the Greeks and Romans* (London, 1775).

Loudon, John Claudius, *Encyclopaedia of Cottage, Farm, and Villa Architecture and Furniture* (London, 1846).

Loudon, John Claudius (ed.), *The Architectural Magazine and Journal* (London, 1834).

Loudon, John Claudius (ed.), *The Architectural Magazine and Journal* (London, 1835).

Mammon, 'How to Urn a Living', *The Observer*, 24 October 1971, p. 25.

Moubray, Amicia de, 'The Secret Coade Unlocked', *Country Life* (27 March 2003), pp. 106-107.

Mowl, Timothy, *Gentlemen & Players* (Stroud, 2000).

Mowl, Timothy and Clare Hickman, *Northamptonshire* (Stroud, 2008).

Parissien, Steven, *Adam Style* (London, 1992).

Parissien, Steven, *Palladian Style* (London, 1994).

Pincot, Daniel, *An Essay on the Origin, Nature, Uses, and Properties, of Artificial Stone* (London, 1770).

Plumtre, George, *Garden Ornament* (London, 1989).

Prudon, Theodore, 'Simulating Stone, 1860-1940', *The Journal of Preservation Technology*, Vol. XXI, Nos. 3/4 (1989), pp. 79-91.

Pulham, James, *Picturesque Rock Garden Scenery, &c.* (London, c1877).

Pulham, James, *Garden Ornament* (London, c1925).

Pulham & Son, 'Advertisement', The Times (26 February 1927), p. 6.

Richardson, Margaret & Stevens, MaryAnne, (eds.) *John Soane Architect* (London, 1999).

Rose, Graham, *The Traditional Garden Book* (London, 1989).

Rowe, Anne (ed.), *Hertfordshire Garden History* (Hatfield, 2007).

Rowland, Tom, 'Nice Little Urns Grow Money for Owners', *The Daily Telegraph* (11 May 1992), p. 4.

Royal Horticultural Society, *Catalogue of Chelsea Show 1972* (Rochester, 1972).

Ruch, John, 'Regency Coade: a Study of the Coade Record Books, 1813-21' in J. Mordaunt Crook (ed.), *Architectural History*, Vol. 11 (1968), pp. 34-56.

Salmon, Frank, *Building on Ruins* (Aldershot, 2000).

Scott, Patricia, *Pottery in Lambeth – a Select Bibliography* (Lambeth, 1976).

Scott, Simon (ed.), *Haddonstone News*, Numbers 1-50 (Northampton, 1993-2008).

Shenstone, William, *The Works in Verse and Prose* (London, 1764).

Smith, John, David Heeley and James Heeson, *Blashfield's – the History, Suggested Guidelines and Ideas for its Regeneration* (Stamford, 2000).

Smith, Louisa, 'Cast Stone: a Genuine Alternative', *Listed Heritage* (September/October 2007), pp. 50-51.

Stanley, Chris and Gillian Bond, *Concrete through the Ages* (Crowthorne, 1999).

Stuart, David, *Georgian Gardens* (London 1979).

Stuart, James, *Critical Observations on the Buildings and Improvements of London* (London, 1771).

Summerson, John, *The Classical Language of Architecture* (London, 1980).

Summerson, John, *The Architecture of the Eighteenth Century* (London, 1986).

Summerson, John, *Architecture in Britain 1530-1830* (New Haven & London, 1993).

Symes, Michael, *A Glossary of Garden History* (Princes Risborough, 1993).

Tatham, Charles, *Etchings of Ancient Ornamental Architecture Drawn from the Originals in Rome and Other Parts of Italy* (London, 1799).

Tournikiotis, Panayotis, *The Historiography of Modern Architecture* (Cambridge, Massachusetts, 1999).

United Kingdom Cast Stone Association, *Research Study into the Development of a Standard Test Method and Performance Specification for Cast Stone* (Crowthorne, 2000).

United Kingdom Cast Stone Association, *Technical Manual for Cast Stone* (2004).

Wade, Tally, 'Haddonstone Cast-Limestone Factory', *AJ Specification* (February 2008), pp. 10-12.

Wagner, Charles and Ian McCaig, 'Cast Stone', *Traditional Homes* (October 1987), pp. 10-20.

Wales, HRH The Prince of, *A Vision of Britain* (London, 1989).

Walpole, Horace, *The History of the Modern Taste in Gardening* (New York, 1995).

Walpole, Horace, *Anecdotes of Painting* (London, 1798).

Watkins, John and Tom Wright (eds.), *The Management & Maintenance of Historic Parks, Gardens & Landscapes* (London, 2007).

Watson, John, *Cements and Artificial Stone* (Cambridge, 1922).

Werff, Rupert van der and Jackie Rees, *Garden Antiques* (London, 2003).

Wilson, Richard & Mackley, Alan, *Creating Paradise* (London & New York, 2000).

Wood, John, *An Essay Towards a Description of Bath* (London, 1749).

Woodcroft, Bennet, *Subject-matter Index (made from titles only) of Patents of Invention, from March 2, 1617 (14 James I) to October 1, 1852 (16 Victoria)* (London, 1857).

Worsley, Giles, *Classical Architecture in Britain* (New Haven & London, 1995).

Worsley, Giles, 'Is Architecture Going Back to the Sixties?', *Daily Telegraph* Arts & Books (11 November 2000), p. 11.

Wyatt, Parker & Co., *Figures, Vases, Fountains &c* (London, 1841).

Yorke, F.R.S., 'Concrete and Artificial Stone', *Architects' Journal* (1 June 1932), pp. 725-729.

Yuille, Robert, 'Artificial Stone Rejected on Extension', *Planning* (19 October 2007), p. 21.

Web Sources

Anon., 'Coade's Artificial Stone Works', *British History Online*, *www.british-history.ac.uk/report.aspx?compid= 47044&strquery=Coade* (accessed 5 June 2007).

Chilstone, 'Material Specification', *www.Chilstone.com/Info_Sheets/Tech6_Material%20Specification.htm* (accessed 5 February 2008)

Clement, Alexander James, 'Sir Henry Doulton', *Oxford Dictionary of National Biography*, *www.oxforddnb.com/view/ printable/7944* (accessed 22 October 2007).

Haddonstone, 'Inspirations', *www.haddonstone.com* (accessed 6 September 2007)

Hesway Limited, 'Creditsafe Online Credit Report', *www1.creditsafeuk.com* (accessed 20 August 2007)

Hesway Limited, 'Creditsafe Online Credit Report', *www1.creditsafeuk.com* (accessed 5 February 2008)

Hitching, Claude, 'The Pulham Legacy', *www.pulham.org.uk* (accessed 22 September 2004).

Ibstock Hathernware, 'Company History', *www.hathernware.co.uk/company/history.htm* (accessed 19 September 2007).

Ibstock Hathernware, 'Products', *www.hathernware.co.uk/products/products-frame.htm* (accessed 19 September 2007).

Iovine, Julie, 'A Discreet Ornamentalism', *New York Times*, http://query.nytimes.com/gst/fullpage.html?res= 9E06E2DE153DF935A35753C1A96 (accessed 1 May 2008).

Kelly, Alison, 'Eleanor Coade', *Oxford Dictionary of National Biography, www.oxforddnb.com/view/printable/37296* (accessed 19 October 2007).

Oxford Dictionary of National Biography, *www.oxforddnb.com* (accessed 19 October 2007).

Smith, John, 'John Marriott Blashfield', *Oxford Dictionary of National Biography*, *www.oxforddnb.com/view/printable/49435* (accessed 19 October 2007).

Steggles, Mary Ann, 'John Bacon', *Oxford Dictionary of National Biography, www.oxforddnb.com/articles/0/994-article. html?back=,37296* (accessed 19 October 2007).

Steptrack Limited, 'Creditsafe Online Credit Report', *www1.creditsafeuk.com* (accessed 5 February 2008)

Thomason Cudworth, *www.coadestone.com* (accessed 31 July 2007)

United Kingdom Cast Stone Association, *www.ukcsa.co.uk* (accessed 17 October 2007).